HIDDEN HISTORY *of*
RHODE ISLAND
AND THE
CIVIL WAR

Hidden History *of*
RHODE ISLAND
AND THE
CIVIL WAR

FRANK L. GRZYB

THE
History
PRESS

Published by The History Press
Charleston, SC 29403
www.historypress.net

Cover images: Image of Battle of Fredericksburg on front courtesy the Providence Public Library Special Collections. Images on back courtesy the Library of Congress.

First published 2013

Manufactured in the United States

ISBN 978.1.62619.231.7

Library of Congress CIP data applied for.

In honor of all departed veterans from Rhode Island units who served during America's Civil War.

And with heartfelt gratitude to the descendants who fight to keep their ancestors' sacrifices and contributions alive.

CONTENTS

PREFACE

While researching material for my previous book, I kept stumbling on stories about Rhode Island's participation in America's Civil War, along with accounts about the conflict that surfaced years later. Some of the tales had been published more than a century ago only to fade into obscurity. In the case of more familiar stories repeated time and again, fresh material has surfaced that suggested a retelling of the stories, especially during the American Civil War Sesquicentennial. Did you know that General Ambrose E. Burnside's personal valet is buried in Rhode Island? That John Wilkes Booth's supposed fiancée met him in Newport only days before he killed the president? That Abraham Lincoln visited Rhode Island but never as president of the United States? That the U.S. Naval Academy was moved from Annapolis to Newport during the war? Or that a Rhode Island lass openly served as a female soldier in the Union army and as a veteran was granted full membership in the Grand Army of the Republic? These and similar stories about Rhode Island and the Civil War can be found within.

Sit back, relax, kick your shoes off and enjoy the ride. You may be pleasantly surprised at what you learn about Rhode Island, the smallest state of the Union, and its ties to the Civil War.

ACKNOWLEDGEMENTS

This is my fourth book, and in many ways, it has become one of the most enjoyable, exhilarating and rewarding assignments I have pursued in years. Finding interesting Civil War stories with Rhode Island ties, checking facts, writing and smoothing them and bringing them to fruition has been a labor of love helped along appreciably by the likes of Dr. Stephen Altic, DO; historian Henry A.L. Brown; and authors Mark H. Dunkelman, James Garman, Robert Grandchamp, Les Rolston, Heath Twichell and Fred Zillian. Also adding significantly to the effort were William Camara of the Rhode Island Veterans Home, Jordan Goffin of the Providence Public Library Special Collections department, Lori Urso of the Pettaquamscutt Historical Society and Brigadier General Richard J. Valente, USA (Ret). Last but not least, I would like to extend a special thanks to my lovely wife, Ginny, a faculty member in the continuing education program at a local college, for her outstanding editorial assistance during the initial draft process. Nobody said it would be easy, but through the support of these mentioned here, more often than not, it seemed that way.

Part I
IN THE BEGINNING

MISCELLANY

Officially called the State of Rhode Island and Providence Plantations, residents of Little Rhody (as it is affectionately referred to by many inhabitants) always seemed to have their own mindset. Banned from the Massachusetts Bay Colony because his religious views substantially differed from the Church of England, Roger Williams founded the colony of Rhode Island in 1636. His religious doctrine was based on the premise that religion and government could peaceably coexist. The doctrine of "separation of church and state" (at the time, such thoughts bordered on blasphemy) is the foundation that we as Americans enjoy today: religious tolerance and freedom.

Roger Williams died in 1683, but his ideals lived on. Nearly a century later, colonists faced another challenge: the right of self-determination. Principals from most of the colonies met in Philadelphia, Pennsylvania, to establish their rights over British occupation and tyranny. At least two conventions met before a plurality was achieved. On September 17, 1787, a constitution was drafted, but before the document could become official, it required the approval of nine of the original thirteen colonies. Delaware became the first to ratify the Constitution on December 7, 1787. Although

Rhode Island was the first state to declare its independence from Great Britain on May 4, 1776, when the time came to send delegates to the Constitutional Convention, it balked, not once but three times. In March 1788, Rhode Island put the issue up for public referendum. The vote failed. When advised that the state would be treated no different than any other foreign government, Rhode Islanders, now feeling cornered, convened a ratification convention. This time, the measure was approved, but only by a slim two-vote margin. On May 29, 1790, Rhode Island became the last state to ratify the Constitution.

Although Rhode Island was the smallest state in size during the Civil War, it never suffered an inferiority complex. Rhode Island's contributions to the war effort were many. Helped along by hardworking immigrants, the state had developed a large industrial base, especially in the textile industry that greatly aided the Union war effort. Rifles and cannons were also produced in abundance. And when President Lincoln called for troops to quell the rebellion, Rhode Island was the first to respond on April 18, 1861, with an infantry unit and a battery of artillery: the First Regiment Rhode Island Detached Militia and the First Light Battery Rhode Island Volunteers. In the ensuing years, the state mustered eight infantry regiments, three cavalry regiments, nine batteries of artillery and three heavy artillery regiments. All were composed predominantly of Rhode Island men.

When the war ended, from a population of about 175,000, Rhode Island had sent 25,236 civilians off to war, sacrificing 1,685 (491 killed in action) of its brave lads to preserve the Union. Soldiers from the state had been present at all the major battles and numerous skirmishes less known today; 16 received the Medal of Honor, 9 of whom were artillerymen. Of the 9, 7 were awarded to members of Battery G, First Regiment Rhode Island Light Artillery, for extraordinary bravery at Petersburg (no U.S. Army battery since has received as many for a single day's engagement). Amazingly, Rhode Island supported Lincoln's repeated calls for troops on every occasion, and when the draft was enacted, it never resorted to conscription, having achieved its quota on each occasion.

Perhaps not as well known, Rhode Island was the first state to issue a call for enlistment of black soldiers in the Union army. The Fourteenth Regiment Rhode Island Heavy Artillery (Colored) was made up of not only Rhode Islanders but also black men from other free states.

Reverend Obadiah Holmes and His Unique Gift to the War Effort

The Rhode Island connection began with Reverend Obadiah Holmes back in the early seventeenth century. Although Reverend Holmes had been dead and buried long before the first shots were fired on Fort Sumter, his legacy continued throughout the Civil War—and, for that matter, for years thereafter.

Who was this man, and what was his connection to our nation? The answer is straightforward: although Reverend Holmes's contribution was significant, his link to the Civil War remains largely unknown. Even in Middletown, Rhode Island, where his role is noted on a small bronze tablet placed within yards of his grave, only a scant few know of his life's work, pious deeds and lasting gift. In fact, in the mid-twentieth century, a wreath was laid and a special tribute paid at the small family cemetery where his remains have rested for several centuries. Witnessed by local dignitaries, Major General Ulysses S. Grant III, grandson of General Ulysses S. Grant, had the honor of placing the wreath next to the severely weathered, barely legible slate headstone.

Obadiah Holmes was born in 1606, 1607 or 1610, depending on which account a person wishes to believe. He came to the colonies after marrying Catherine Hyde on November 20, 1630. The ceremony had taken place at Manchester's Collegiate College Church in Lancashire, England. Crossing the Atlantic in 1638 proved to be a long and grueling affair, as he and his wife encountered rough seas and inclement weather throughout their voyage. Not long after landing, the couple traveled north and settled in the small town of Salem. While residing there, Reverend Holmes was admitted to the Church of England. To earn a stable existence, he started the first window glass foundry in the colonies while continuing to pursue his religious calling. But after facing unyielding religious persecution and his inability to curb his outspoken demeanor when it came to his spiritual beliefs, especially those that differed substantially from the Church of England, he was excommunicated from the church. The chastising forced him to move some forty miles south to a small town called Rehoboth.

After preaching his puritanical ideals to a group of locals, he was ordered to abstain from such ministry. Not to be deprived of his convictions and his desire to promote his faith without outside interference, Obadiah and his wife moved again, this time only a short distance to the colony of

The United Baptist Church stands on the site where Reverend Homes founded his first ministry in the colony of Rhode Island. *Photo by the author.*

Rhode Island, where religious teachings such as his were better tolerated. But soon, more problems arose. In 1651, Reverend Holmes decided to return to Massachusetts to help an old man with an undisclosed illness. Unfortunately for Reverend Holmes, he and his two-man party made the mistake of conducting a religious service in the man's home. It was not long before local spiritual leaders got wind of the heresy and placed him under arrest. Fined thirty pounds, Reverend Holmes refused to pay, preferring the dire consequences of a public flogging.

On September 5, 1651, in Boston, Massachusetts, Reverend Holmes, after being tied to a whipping post, took the thirty lashes with neither a groan nor a scream. It was not an easy punishment at the hands of the punisher, who was said to flail a three-cord whip using both hands simultaneously to achieve the full force of each blow. Accounts note that between lashes, Reverend Holmes continued to preach his beliefs to the crowd. Although the flogging swiftly curbed his strength, he was heard to say, "You have struck me as with roses." After paying for his indiscretions with a pound of flesh, Reverend Holmes was forced to remain in Boston until he recovered several weeks later. In the meantime, he ate his meals on his hands and knees like a dog until the cuts began to heal and the pain in his back subsided. His suffering so impressed Bostonians that a Baptist church was founded there soon after his departure.

In 1652, and following in the religious footsteps of a colleague, Roger Williams, Reverend Holmes became the pastor of the First Baptist Church in Newport, Rhode Island. There he succeeded his friend and first pastor, Reverend John Clarke. For some thirty years, his ministry continued as his church grew in size and stature.

During his life, Reverend Holmes fathered nine children and forty-two grandchildren. When he passed away in 1682, he left a legacy of spirituality for his children by instructing them to live their lives according to scripture and to "meet, support, strengthen, and reprove one another."

Six generations passed before Reverend Holmes's unique gift found its way to a person both adored as a saint and loathed as a devil, depending on which side of the Civil War one stood. What was the gift this humble and pious man bequeathed to a generation facing the worst war the United States ever experienced? Reverend Obadiah Holmes never knew and perhaps never envisioned that his genes would find their way into the body of one our nation's greatest presidents: Abraham Lincoln. Indeed, Abraham Lincoln was his direct descendent.

For those interested in the lineage, this is how it came to pass:

- Obadiah Holmes (16??–1682) married Catherine Hyde;
- Their daughter Lydia Holmes (????–1693) married John Bowne (1530–1684);
- Their daughter Sarah Bowne (1669–1714) married Richard Salter (????–1728);
- Their daughter Hannah Salter (????–1727) married Mordecai Lincoln (1686–1736);
- Their son John Lincoln (1716–1788) married Rebecca Flowers (1720–1806);
- Their son Abraham Lincoln (1744–1786) married Bathsheba Herring (?) (1750–1836);
- Their son Thomas Lincoln (1778–1851) married Nancy Hanks (1784–1851); and
- Their son Abraham Lincoln married Mary Todd. Years later, Lincoln became the sixteenth president of the United States of America.

Plaque imbedded in the ground at the Rhode Island Historical Cemetery in Middletown, Rhode Island, that commemorates Reverend Holmes. *Photo by the author.*

Did Abraham Lincoln know of his ancestry and New England roots? It is doubtful. Lincoln once professed to not knowing who his grandfather was, much less having a Baptist minister in his family tree many generations removed.

For those curious, if given the opportunity to visit the town of Middletown, Rhode Island, on picturesque Aquidneck Island, it is worth a short detour from the center of the business district to see the Holmes Burial Ground, the official designation of which is the Rhode Island Historical Cemetery, Middletown, No. 19. Near the road is a small bronze plaque attached to a slab of granite that denotes Reverend Obadiah Holmes's foremost accomplishments. His final resting place lies only yards away.

ABRAHAM LINCOLN VISITS RHODE ISLAND

Abraham Lincoln came to Rhode Island on three separate occasions—not as president of the United States, but undoubtedly with presidential aspirations in mind. In September 1848, Lincoln stopped in the capital city of Providence on his way to a Whig Party convention in Worcester, Massachusetts. After a short layover, he departed for New Bedford. Then, in 1860, and now a Republican, he made overnight visits to Rhode Island. Campaigning for the nation's highest office was foremost in Lincoln's mind, as was the opportunity to visit his son Robert, a student at prestigious Phillips Academy in Exeter, New Hampshire.

Initially, Lincoln planned to speak about the country's most pressing issue of slavery to an audience in Brooklyn, New York. The talk was eventually moved from Brooklyn to Cooper Institute in Manhattan to accommodate a larger audience, which would include such notables as William Cullen Bryant, Horace Greeley and David Dudley Field. Knowing the difficult challenge that lay ahead in his campaign due to his limited political exposure outside the Midwest, Lincoln spent nearly three days honing his speech before actually giving it on February 27, 1860.

When Lincoln arrived at the institute, his physical appearance surprised many in attendance. He was unlike anything the spectators had imagined. An attendee described him thusly:

> *Mr. Lincoln was a tall man about 40 years of age, clothed in dark clothing with a black silk cravat, over six feet in height, slightly stooping as tall men sometimes are, with long arms, which he frequently moved in gesticulation, of dark complexion with dark almost black hair, with strong and homely features, with sad eyes, which moved in earnest argument or quiet humor, and then assumed a calm sadness.*

Soon, however, his words overwhelmed the influential crowd. His speech that day became a classic and today is celebrated as "Lincoln's Cooper Union Address." With methodical reasoning, a persuasive argument and a no-nonsense delivery, his remarks catapulted him to national prominence in the days and weeks ahead. The American press enhanced his rising image with glowing articles about his talk. Arguably, his most memorable words that evening were given in his closing statement: "Let us have faith that right makes might, and in that faith, let us, to the end, dare to do our duty as we understand it."

The following morning, Lincoln departed Manhattan by train, passing northeast through Connecticut and into southern Rhode Island before arriving in Providence late in the afternoon. He was just in time for a dinner engagement at the homestead of Mr. John Eddy, a prominent Rhode Island

In early June 1860, photographer Alexander Hesler traveled from Chicago to Springfield, Illinois, to take Abraham Lincoln's image. *Library of Congress.*

lawyer and local Republican who had accompanied Lincoln on the train. Eddy had recruited Lincoln to speak in Providence while both were in New York. Hours later, Lincoln spoke to an audience estimated at 1,500 on the second floor of Railroad Hall at the northern end of the Union Passenger. (The 1848 building, once touted as the longest of such type in America, has long since been razed, and the Federal Courthouse at Kennedy Plaza is now situated on the site. A bronze plaque is visible on the building—the corner of Exchange Street and Fulton Street—commemorating Lincoln's appearance.) Lincoln's speech that evening was said to be a repeat performance of the previous evening. Unfortunately, the hall was not large enough, and many were turned away, although a contingent of students from Brown University did gain access. Among them was William Ide Brown. Five years later, while fighting for the Union, Brown was killed at Petersburg.

After an introduction by Honorable Thomas A. Jencks, Lincoln took the floor. His opening remarks alluded to items he had read in a newspaper while traveling by train to the city. The speech was slightly different then the speech he gave at Cooper Institute the previous evening, but according to local press, there appeared to be many similarities. His oration lasted two and a half hours, and unfortunately, no transcription of his talk has been found. As was to be expected, Lincoln's words met with mixed reviews, depending on the political persuasion of the local press. The *Providence Daily Journal*, the Republican newspaper, commended his efforts, while the more conservative democratic newspaper, the *Providence Daily Post*, was less than kind. Neither commentary came as a surprise. By most accounts, gains were made by Lincoln that evening that swayed more citizens from Rhode Island to his side of the slavery argument: that he and his party were against the expansion of slavery in the territories and that slavery could not be defended by the U.S. Constitution.

Following his successful speech, Lincoln spent the remainder of the day at the home of his host, in a house located in a residential neighborhood on Washington Street. Mr. Eddy, a merchant and prominent lawyer in Providence, was the brother-in-law of Charles T. James, owner of a number of cotton mills and a former Democratic U.S. senator from the state (James's exploits are covered later in another story). Meeting Mr. Eddy's wife must have been a pleasure, but encountering Eddy's four-year-old child, Alfred, may have been better. Lincoln loved children and always seemed prepared for such occasions. Fetching a handful of red gumdrops from his pocket, he handed them to the young boy. The thoughtful gift made a lasting impression on Alfred. As years passed and Alfred grew old, his memories of Lincoln's visit remained crystallized in his memory.

Harris Hall as it appears today. Lincoln spoke on the third floor, top right, that today serves as the town council chamber. *Photo by the author.*

Mr. Eddy, being a tall man, had a bed manufactured to fit his own elongated proportions. Lincoln was extended the privilege of sleeping on the bed that night. When awoke in the morning, Lincoln was quick to compliment his host on the comfortable arrangements (a dated account states that the bed Lincoln slept in and the chair where he sat was preserved by descendants of the family). No doubt, this bed was an exception to the rule when he hit the campaign trail.

After his Providence speech, two Woonsocket, Rhode Island businessmen—Lattimer W. Ballou, founder of the Republican Party in Rhode Island, and Edward Harris, a Rhode Island industrialist— approached Lincoln about speaking in their city after his return trip from visiting his eldest son, Robert, in New Hampshire. Lincoln savored the opportunity to expand his political base in Rhode Island. Realizing that he was somewhat of an unknown quantity in New England and being politically savvy, he accepted the invitation.

The following morning, Lincoln woke and proceeded to board a northbound train to Boston. From here, he traveled to New Hampshire.

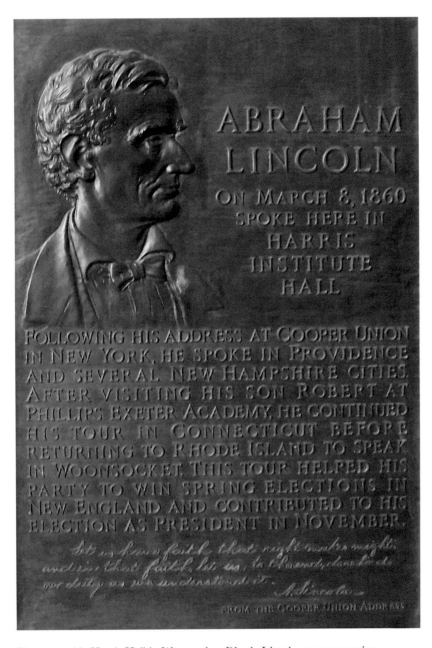

Plaque outside Harris Hall in Woonsocket, Rhode Island, commemorating Abraham Lincoln's speech. *Photo by the author.*

There, he visited Robert at Phillips Academy. The subsequent conversation that transpired between the two remains a mystery but probably included talk about family, Robert's schooling and his future aspirations.

Upon his return trip by rail, Lincoln's journey took him through Providence, but he never disembarked. After a brief layover, the train departed for New Haven, Connecticut, where Lincoln gave another speech. However, as promised, in less than a week, Lincoln returned to Rhode Island to deliver a rousing speech at Harris Hall in Woonsocket, now the site of city hall. Little is known about the content of his talk, but accounts allude to similarities with his Cooper Union oration. A noted Woonsocket manufacturer, Darius Farnum, noted in his diary soon after the speech: "Presidential campaign for Republican party for 1860 opened in Woonsocket tonight by Honorable Abraham Lincoln of Illinois—a very tall spare man." After the speech, Lincoln spent the night at the Harris house. In commemoration of the speech, a bronze plaque similar to the one in Providence has been affixed outside the entry door of the building. The following day, March 9, Lincoln left Rhode Island for his home in Springfield, Illinois. He never returned to the state, but he might have had it not been for an assassin's bullet.

As for the young child who was given gumdrops by Abraham Lincoln, he grew up to attend Brown University (class of 1879), where he became the first captain of the football team. Three years after graduation, he founded the Mercantile Mutual Fire Insurance Company, serving on the board of directors until his death. During his lifetime, Eddy relished the opportunity to reminisce about his childhood meeting with the future president. How much he accurately remembered about Lincoln's visit to his homestead is questionable. What he had seen that day may have been retold and reinforced by his parents as he grew older. Arguably, he certainly had an interesting tale to relate during his lifetime. Alfred Updike Eddy lived to a ripe old age, passing away three months shy of his eighty-first birthday.

Today, a statue of President Abraham Lincoln can be seen in Roger Williams Park, Providence. The monument is the only effigy of Lincoln in the entire state.

RALLYING CRIES HEARD
THROUGHOUT THE STATE

In less than six months, eleven Southern states did what Northerners thought would never happen: they seceded from the Union. Aristocratic Southerners believed that by forming their own country, they would preserve slavery, states' rights, political liberty and what was particularly important to them, Southern honor. One after another, each rebellious state became part of the Confederate States of America under newly elected provisional president Jefferson Davis (in November of the same year, Davis was elected to a permanent six-year term).

Astonishingly, the Confederacy based its constitution on many of the same principles on which the nation it seceded from was founded. It organized its own army and navy, enlisting men who were students, instructors or graduates of the U.S. Military Academy, U.S. Naval Academy and from lesser-known military schools in the South. It issued its own currency, largely without sufficient assets to back up its monetary value. But the Confederacy was a determined group of men and women feeling destined to succeed in what would become a difficult and costly struggle. In the end, achieving the dream proved insurmountable. In the North, well-established manufacturing concerns, seemingly unlimited financial resources and a large population to muster and resupply an army proved to be the South's undoing. But it did not start that way. Southern optimism ran high, and there were no thoughts other than complete victory.

In the North, the majority of citizens were appalled by the rebellion. There were Copperheads, of course—those who lived in the North but sympathized with the Southern cause. And like any nation facing the turmoil of a civil war, there were citizens eager to profit. But the average citizen in the North felt an allegiance to the Union. Northern newspapers ran editorials condemning the South's move to secede, calling the reasons for succession "sophism"—a seldom-used word today meaning a plausible but fallacious argument. Northerners were convinced that the Southern states had no basis to dissolve the Union.

But even after the capture of Fort Sumter in Charleston, South Carolina, by the Confederates, nearly every Northerner felt that the war would be short-lived; that supposition—both highly optimistic and extremely naïve—proved to be a grave miscalculation. Local militias and those eager to strike a blow against the rebellious states prepared to fight in droves. Because the war would be over in a heartbeat, or so many thought, there was little need to muster regiments for military service longer than ninety days. Rhode Island was no exception.

Recruitment broadsides. Top left: *Office of the Secretary of State, A. Ralph Mollis, Rhode Island State Archives*. Top right and bottom: *Providence Marine Corps of Artillery*.

Throughout the North, war rallies were held frequently, especially in early to mid-1861. Mayors, military contingents, state and local politicians and dignitaries—even clergy—served as speakers working large crowds into frenzies. The meetings, usually held at city and town halls and squares, became regularly scheduled events, much attended and a welcomed respite for those who toiled during the workweek. Some looked on these meetings as jovial affairs, much like the community picnics that were enormously popular during the period. In the final analysis, rallies served to fuel the passion and patriotism of those in attendance, as well as, more importantly, recruiting drives and fundraisers to pay for local enlistment bonuses.

In Rhode Island, broadsides were posted on virtually every street corner and town hall, announcing the date and location of the next war rally. State and local newspapers ran bylines publicizing the event and reinforcing the need for everyone's attendance. On Aquidneck Island, a tight-knit community made up of three towns—Newport, Middletown and Portsmouth—William Cranston, mayor of Newport, usually led the proceedings. During one afternoon rally in the city, an American flag was raised on the liberty pole under which was erected a speaker's rostrum "profusely decorated with the flags of various nations tastefully festooned in four triangular directions from the central point." Several hundred holiday-attired citizens heard the Naval Band play patriotic marches as midshipmen fired cannon salvos from the USS *Constitution* (affectionately known as "Old Ironsides"), moored in the harbor. No records exist as to the amount of money received or how many men enlisted, but from what was printed in the local newspaper, the event appeared to be a resounding success.

In neighboring Bristol, a town meeting was held on Saturday, May 18, 1861, to "aid the volunteer company in filling up their ranks." A flag was raised, patriotic songs sung, letters read and "soul-stirring arguments and truths set forth by the speakers," and a letter written by a local citizen was also read aloud that ended with the simplest of wishes: "That the noble effort of our patriotic volunteers to fill their ranks…be successful."

Near the end of July 1861, after the Union's humiliating loss at Bull Run, politicians and high-ranking dignitaries held a late morning recruitment rally at Market Square in Providence. The purpose of the gathering was "to give opportunity for the people to express their feelings in regard to the recent disaster to a portion of our army, and to encourage each other to more resolute and energetic action." In the end, the men unanimously adopted the following resolution:

That in this hour of disaster we recognize our duty to our country; and that we pledge anew our fortunes and our lives to uphold the national government, to maintain the integrity of the national territory, and to preserve the national honor.

During the same week of the Market Square rally, citizens of Providence welcomed the First Regiment Rhode Island Volunteer Infantry back from the front. Considering the celebration, a person would have thought the Union had won the battle. At 6:30 a.m. on a Sunday, Union soldiers were greeted by thousands of citizens at the wharf to a "hearty welcome" of cheers and applause. After speeches were made and a grand salute fired, the regiment marched to the main armory, led by General Ambrose E. Burnside. It was said that the path back to the Benefit Street Armory was paved with bouquets thrown by appreciative ladies. At the armory, the regiment was served a breakfast but not before listening to more patriotic speeches.

Fresh from the battlefield, Burnside began to make appearances at several rallies throughout the state. On the first Tuesday in August 1861, Burnside and his staff visited Newport. After arriving on the steamer *Perry*, the general and his entourage were escorted by the American Brass Band of Providence and the Naval Academy Band to Touro Park. Burnside was again greeted by a shower of bouquets. Mayor William Cranston gave the introductory remarks before presenting the honored guest with a ceremonial sword. Saying a few words of appreciation, Burnside accepted the sword, begged leave and then retired to a buffet at the Fillmore House.

Back in Providence, another rally was held at the town hall on Monday evening, September 16, 1861. Newspapers reported that the hall was overflowing with curious citizens, including "a number of patriotic ladies." There was no secret agenda. It was held to "induce our young men to enter the service of their country." The usual speakers were in attendance, but this time Governor William Sprague "made a few practical remarks" that impressed many a young man in the crowd. Three days later, a similar rally was held at the same location.

Back in April, the rallies often ended with the cry: "War! War! War!" By the beginning of September, the sentiment had shifted somewhat. Citizens of Rhode Island as well as all the other Union states began to realize that the war might be a long, drawn-out affair. Little did they imagine the extent of the carnage yet to come.

Down South

Originally from Prussia, one eighteen-year-old Rhode Islander experienced a different perspective about secession than the average Northerner could have ever imagined. William E. Meyer not only saw but also heard the bigotry and hatred railed against black men from one of his own superiors. Serving onboard the one-hundred-ton centerboard schooner *Harriet Lewis* out of Newport, Rhode Island, Meyer gained a startling insight about Southern rights and slavery while serving as a crewmember. Although the experience solidified his position as a Union man, it came at an expense: genuine fear for his own safety.

The crew of the *Harriet Lewis* had been warned while sailing past Hampton Roads, Virginia, by a U.S. naval officer onboard a vessel anchored nearby in the bay: "Norfolk is in a very unsettled state. You may go in, but you may not come out again with a whole skin." The captain on Meyer's schooner decided not to heed the warning, as war between the two factions was as yet undeclared, and because there were only intermittent disturbances reported in the city, many onboard felt that the unrest would quickly subside. The following day, a towboat came out to escort them to a designated wharf.

Not long after arrival, the crew unloaded the cargo of molasses from Havana, Cuba, near a massive U.S. naval yard. The unloading went without incident. That night, and without fear, much of the crew disembarked to spend time on land, as sailors normally do when in port. Young Meyer decided to stay aboard. What he heard in the distance while on deck that night rattled him. As Meyer reported later, "Wild crowds, yelling, hooting in mad haste would race with their hand engines from other points; they stopped, connected [the] fire hose and pumped high sprays of sparkling water over trees and housetops, but no fire [was] yet in sight." *What did it mean?*, he thought. He answered his own question: "The 'Devil was let loose in Norfolk,' and had crazed the people into madness; beer [and] liquor flowed freely from the corner rum shops." There were cheers for Jeff Davis by one and then the multitude. *But who was Jeff Davis?*, Meyer wondered.

Days later, the naval yard was ablaze. A number of Virginia militia entered the city, and two thousand cannons reportedly fell into Southern hands. The mob had not only seized the naval yard but was also in the process of taking over "Yankee schooners" at the dock and in the harbor. That night, although the *Harriet Lewis* was not boarded, its crew, along with young Meyer, was now in a precarious position.

Much to Meyer's dismay, the following morning several key members of the crew announced that they had joined the Confederate navy, "that good jobs were awaiting them…and invited us to be 'men' and to come along and join the fortunes of war." Their final advice to the Northern crew was to leave the schooner before it was sunk in the channel. A decision had already been made to do just that to prevent Yankee warships from entering the port. The departure by the recently "converted" Confederate sailors was seen as nothing short of treason by those remaining loyal to the Union. But their views and allegiance did not come as a surprise, especially to Meyer. Back in 1860, he overheard a conversation between the ship's captain, Williams, and a Mr. Ladd, the gist of which was that "black men had no soul and therefore, no soul to save."

As the days dragged on, with the *Harriet Lewis* still in port, Meyer not only saw but could also feel the Southern sentiment against Northerners. As he explained, "Woe to the man who dared to express an opinion contrary to the general feeling." Meyer witnessed thousands of bales of cotton stacked for breastworks, while armed men placed rifles behind them. Over the sound of martial music, rioting men were heard ranting and raving.

Meyer's schooner now became a target for "aggressively blasphemous remarks and disagreeable missiles falling on side and deck from passing junk and bumboat men." The decision was made by a superior: using dark paint, Meyer was ordered to cover the name *Harriet Lewis* and the words "Newport, R.I.," painted on the stern and the side quarter boards of the vessel. According to Meyer, the task brought him "better peace and comfort."

That night brought fair winds, and a decision was made to hoist the sails. Using the tide and wind, the *Harriet Lewis* departed the hostile port city. By daybreak, the vessel and crew were miles away, but not without incident—a cannon shot had ripped through the mainsail from a shore battery.

TRASH TALK

America's Civil War was far from a sporting event, but if you read the trash talk between the two contenders, you might think otherwise. Case in point is the following advertisement, which was placed in an Augusta, Georgia, newspaper sometime around March or April of 1861:

500 Washer Women with broomsticks to whip back Governor Sprague's regiment from Rhode Island lately offered to Lincoln.

Using byline space instead of an advertisement in its newspaper, the *Providence Journal* responded in kind:

That is the way the Georgians propose to fight. We had heard their valor doubted, but did not suppose they would call upon the women to begin fighting for them.

Newspaper jabs between both sides became increasingly personal and vindictive as the war progressed. To say which side at any given moment instigated the attack is difficult. Newspapers both North and South did their fair share to aggravate the other side. Perhaps the best decision is to call it a draw.

But if anything is learned from all this, perhaps "trash talk" should be included as another American Civil War first placed right up there with Thaddeus Lowe's first aerial reconnaissance with his balloon. After all, both require an abundance of hot air, right?

PRACTICAL ADVICE TO NEW RECRUITS

The Saturday, April 27, 1861 edition of the *Bristol Phenix* in Bristol, Rhode Island, repeated some advice to volunteers that had been previously published in the *New York Post*. The words of wisdom came from an old veteran:

Remember that in a campaign more men die from sickness than by the bullet.

Line your blanket with one thickness of brown drilling. This adds but four ounces in weight, and doubles the warmth.

Buy a small India rubber blanket (only $1.50) to lay on the ground or to throw over your shoulders when on guard duty during a rain storm. Most of the eastern troops are provided with these. Straw to lie upon is not always to be had.

The best military hat in use is the light colored soft felt, the crown being sufficiently high to allow space for air over the brain. You can fasten it up as a continental in fair weather or turn it down when it is wet or very sunny.

Let your beard grow, so as to protect the throat and lungs.

Keep your entire person clean: this prevents fevers and bowel complaints in warm climates. Wash your body each day, if possible. Avoid strong coffee and oily meat. General Scott said that the too free use of these (together with neglect in keeping the skin clean) cost many a soldier his life in Mexico.

A sudden check of perspiration by chilly or night air often causes fever and death. When thus exposed do not forget your blanket.

For prospective soldiers sensible enough to heed the advice, the article was not only timely and insightful but also potentially lifesaving.

AN INAUSPICIOUS BEGINNING

Recruits of newly formed batteries within the state first drilled at the old armory of the Providence Marine Corps of Artillery on Benefit Street in the capital city. Here they learned the fundamental lessons of artillerymen: marching, facing, forming detachments and practicing the manual of the piece pertaining to artillery drills. Soon they became quite adept at all of the above, but that was within the confines of the armory. Anxious to perform outdoor field drills, a newly formed battery had to wait patiently for uniforms to arrive before the men could perfect their skills under field conditions. Finally they came. Each uniform consisted of a pair of pantaloons (pants), a blouse (shirt) and a high felt hat with one side pinned back by a brass eagle insignia while the front sported a brass insignia of crossed cannons. Because the uniforms were distributed regardless of size, the new recruits exchanged with one another until "they soon made a very respectable appearance."

In August 1861, now in full dress, two detachments of recruits detailed as drivers and cannoneers left the armory and made their way to a nearby park, where they were to take part in initial field maneuvers. Following the parade of men, horses, cannons and caissons were curious bystanders waiting to be entertained by the precision movements of the artillery teams.

After the officers gave instructions regarding the alignment of men, horses and pieces, the first drill commenced. But coordination between drivers of the pieces (cannons) and the drivers of the caissons was far from a well-oiled machine. As the drivers pulled their cannons, the caisson

Top: The Benefit Street Arsenal in Providence. *Library of Congress.* Insert: Bronze plaque affixed to a wall outside the arsenal. *Photo by the author.*

drivers were waiting for what they thought would be a separate command. Frustrated after several attempts to have all move in unison, the lieutenant commanded the recruits "that they must follow the pieces at all times, even if they went to hell."

The caisson drivers learned their lesson well. The team of horses pulling the first cannon was extremely high-spirited, and the drivers were having problems controlling the horses after all the frequent starting and stopping maneuvers. When a subsequent order was given, the horses pulling the cannon wheeled, turned and bolted toward downtown Providence at breakneck speed. The caisson drivers, remembering their orders to "follow the pieces…even if they went to hell," also pulled out of line, whipped and spurred the horses into a full gallop trying to catch up with the runaway team, all while the bewildered lieutenant shouted for the caisson drivers to stop. His attempt was to no avail. In desperation, the lieutenant pursued the runaways on horseback. Those left behind, however, wondered if what they were witnessing was a race, a runaway or some kind of unique drill. After the officer successfully stopped the drivers of the caisson, he asked why they left the line. Innocently they reminded him about his orders. In the meantime, a sergeant sent to retrieve the runaway piece returned with the cannon and a tired but intact group of men and horses.

The rest of the drill did not fare any better. The first day's drill was called off after a second mishap occurred when three men sitting on a limber chest experienced the ride of a lifetime. After drivers attempted to make too tight of a turn, the horses' harness became entangled, and the men sitting on each side of the limber were thrown off. Because the chest had been emptied of substantial weight, the man sitting in the middle had nothing to grasp for support. As the chest tilted backward, the ill-fated recruit proceeded to take a backward somersault landing on his side with his shirt pulled over his head. Uninjured but embarrassed, he was asked about the peculiar maneuver. The recruit said that "he was not in favor of that way for the cannoneers to dismount, and would rather be a driver."

The U.S. Naval Academy during the Civil War

In 1845, Secretary of the Navy George Bancroft helped establish the U.S. Naval Academy in Annapolis, Maryland. But by the spring of 1861, the academy was "in imminent danger of dissolution" due to its precarious location near the rebellious states. Because the border state of Maryland included many Southern sympathizers, Bancroft—a frequent summer resident of Newport, Rhode Island—persuaded members of Congress to move the military establishment to Newport. His motives may have been a bit selfish and perhaps self-evident, as he had personal and business interests in the area. But the fact remained that Annapolis, Maryland, was located in an area with many secessionist sympathizers; it was easily accessible to armed vessels from the Chesapeake, and the site was virtually defenseless from enemy attack on the Baltimore side. Compounding the problem, "Old Ironsides" was docked at the pier near the academy, and fear grew daily that the vessel would be confiscated by secessionists and used as the "nursery of the future southern navy."

In late April 1861, the War Department issued an order temporarily placing the U.S. Naval Academy under the secretary of the navy and ordering its removal to Fort Adams in Newport, Rhode Island. By early

The Atlantic House, home of the U.S. Naval Academy in Newport. *Naval War College Museum.*

May 1861, the staff and midshipmen had sailed to Newport onboard the frigate USS *Constitution* and the steamer *Baltic*. For the first five months, Fort Adams and the USS *Constitution* served as the U.S. Naval Academy for approximately 130 to 140 midshipmen. But this proved to be a transitional move because of several limitations, some of which were health-related. Exceptional as a defensive fortification and for the training of infantry and artillery soldiers, Fort Adams left much to be desired for the proper education of future naval officers. Specifically, the stone fortification was dark, damp and dirty. After a brief search, the former Atlantic House, a hotel on the corner of Pelham Street and fashionable Bellevue Avenue in the center of Newport, was selected as the most feasible location. A lease arrangement between the government and the hotel owner was negotiated.

While still at Fort Adams with the Naval Academy contingent, John C. Pegram recalled an annoying incident. He and his fellow students were visited by local citizens and political dignitaries onboard ship during dining hours and were looked upon as "some strange animals" with a "mixture of disgust and merriment." Pegram overhead an old lady questioning an officer, "Do you give them meat?" Pegram never forgot the incident. He wrote later "that the good old dame judged from our youthful appearance that we ought to be

Two midshipmen at the U.S. Naval Academy in Newport, Rhode Island. *Author's collection.*

restricted to a 'milk' diet, or that from the savage nature of the profession for which we were training we ought to be brought up on rum and gunpowder, was never discovered." But the mood of the community did change, and the midshipmen were accepted by the vast majority.

When alterations were completed at the Atlantic House, classes reconvened at the new campus on September 21, 1861, and here the military educational and training institution remained for the duration of the war. In the years that followed, the midshipmen trained to be good seamen, first-rate gunners, excellent navigators and honorable and outstanding citizens.

Surrounding the U.S. Naval Academy were a number of businesses, including a consortium of photographers that could smell the potential business from the faculty, staff and students at the military establishment. The location was ideal for such a business, as it was centrally located near the commercial district of Newport. The proximity to the academy provided them with a better opportunity to serve their ever-growing clientele interested in sending their images home to family and friends. Joshua Appleby Williams made a respectable living taking photographs of midshipmen at his studio, and so did J.D. Fowler, F. Kindler and a host of other entrepreneurs in the vicinity of the institution.

Across the street from the academy was Touro Park, which served as the formal drill and parade grounds. Going beyond Touro Park was considered off-limits for the midshipmen unless they had permission to venture further.

In October 1862, the USS *Santee* arrived in Newport and was put to service as the school ship. In May of the following year, the schooner-yacht *America* was also assigned to the academy.

In May 1863, Edward Everett gave the commencement address to a class of twenty-one students from the class that had commenced their naval education in 1860 at Annapolis, Maryland. The midshipmen had little time to enjoy the honor as they were immediately ordered into active service. The next autumn, the balance of the 1860 class also graduated, and those men, too, were assigned duties on various vessels.

By the start of 1865, there was much talk among the citizenry as to what would become of the academy now that the end of the war was in sight. Rumors began to fly about the academy moving back to Maryland, and editorial comments filled the *Newport Daily News* almost on a weekly basis with predictions about the educational institution's eventual move south. On the political and military side, there were grave concerns that the academy had become too liberal arts–oriented from its earlier curriculum of more practical training. An investigative board headed by Admiral David G. Farragut was convened to look into the matter. Its findings confirmed what many had already suspected: the move to Newport and the radical changes implemented there were not up to the academy's previous standards. After four years in its temporary home, the academy moved back to Annapolis on August 9, 1865, with Admiral Farragut in charge. The Atlantic House was eventually sold at auction not long after. When classes reconvened at Annapolis, Maryland, the curriculum underwent extensive changes, bringing it more in line with the institution's original training objectives.

The Atlantic House was torn down in 1877 to make way for private residences. Today, all that remains at the site is a sign and plaque near an

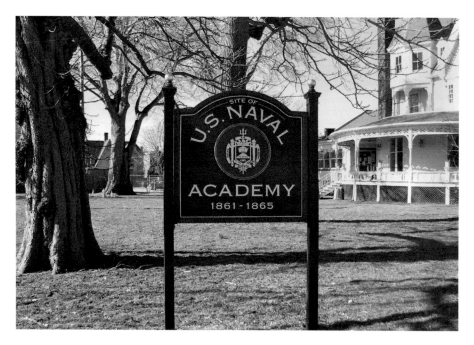

The U.S. Naval Academy was located on this site. The site is now the home of an Elks Lodge. *Photo by the author.*

Elks Lodge commemorating the U.S. Naval Academy's presence in Newport. Although not without problems, the U.S. Naval Academy in Newport continued the proud tradition of grooming the finest officers for its fleet during the Civil War.

JOHN M. HAY: THE EARLY YEARS

Perhaps no other assistant secretary to the president of the United States has had more written about him than John M. Hay. His photographs alongside President Abraham Lincoln have been published in hundreds, if not thousands, of books over the past century and a half. And his accomplishments during his career (both civilian and political) have been well documented. During his illustrious career, Hay served in a variety of diplomatic positions, as a night editor of the *New York Tribune*, as assistant secretary of state and as an ambassador to Great Britain under President William McKinley before rising to secretary of state in the same administration. But where did it all begin, and what are the particulars that tie Hay to Rhode Island?

John M. Hay was born on October 8, 1838, in Salem, Indiana. The third child of Dr. Charles and Helen Hay, John's early life was spent in a small, single-story brick house of which he would have no memory later in life. Seeking a better existence, the Hay family moved in 1841 to Warsaw, Illinois, a frontier settlement on the banks of the Mississippi. Here, John and his siblings spent their youth.

During his toddler days, John learned to string words together in rhymes; at the tender age of seven, he was learning German. While still a young boy, he told his brother that he saw and heard a ghost in the basement. According to John, the presumed ghost asked, "Little Master, for the love of God bring me a drink of water." Scared out of his wits, he ran upstairs and locked himself in his room. The next morning, John told his father about the incident. It turns out that John did see and hear something—not a ghost, but rather something that seemed to be an apparition to a young boy's eyes. What he saw and heard was actually a runaway slave who had been wounded during an escape. Dr. Hay, John and John's brother, Leonard, went downstairs and found an area where someone had made a makeshift bed; along it was an eighteen-inch-diameter bloodstain. John never forgot the incident; it solidified his antislavery views for the rest of his life.

When the time came for a primary education, John and his brother were schooled by an Episcopal clergyman. Two of their main subjects were Latin and Greek. In 1851, John was sent to a private academy in Pittsfield, Massachusetts. Here he met John G. Nicolay, six years his elder and a Bavarian by birth. They hit it off immediately, especially because Hay spoke fluent German. Hay and Nicolay became good friends. They would meet again less than a decade later, when each would eventually play significant supporting roles on a much larger stage.

The following year, Hay attended a college in Springfield, Illinois, that was more a preparatory school than a college. With Springfield as the capital and the seat of the state legislature, young Hay would see men like the rotund Senator Stephen A. Douglas and a tall, lanky lawyer who was developing quite a name for himself: Abraham Lincoln. By 1855, Hay was destined for bigger challenges. He had already gained the respect of his classmates. Nonetheless, when time came for celebration, Hay could also saunter with the best; he picnicked, partied and danced. Although young Hay must have had some say about his future education, scholars say that his parents made the decision that he should attend Brown University in Providence, Rhode Island, where Mrs. Hay's father, David Augustus Leonard, had graduated some sixty years earlier. Although founded as a Baptist institution, Brown's charter provided the assurance of a nonsectarian education and "a full, free, absolute, and uninterrupted liberty of conscience"—proudly adhered to today as well.

On Friday, September 7, 1855, just one month shy of his seventeenth birthday, Hay became a member of Brown University's freshman class; the student body consisted of 225 classmates, with nine professors as educators. In a letter home after his safe arrival in Providence, Hay told his parents, "I had a whirling, hustling time on the way here, but at last arrived…safe and sound in everything, except my eyes, mouth and ears were full of cinders and dust." In the following paragraph, he commented about settling in and registering for three classes, "Chemistry, Rhetoric, and Trigonometry." Further, he explained, "We also have exercises in speaking and writing essays." But what is evident in this first letter home from college is Hay's maturity: his willingness to adapt to new surroundings and his desire to grasp the opportunity and succeed intellectually. Hay demonstrated the sense of humor that would sustain him throughout his life when he closed the letter by sending his love to "Grandpa, aunts, uncles, cousins, and cats," adding a postscript, "Somebody write soon—soon—do you hear? SOON."

Hay, like other freshman boarding students, was assigned a "conveniently furnished apartment." His was located in room 19 on the second floor of University Hall, a building that was constructed in 1770. The city he would call home for the next three years was founded by Roger Williams in 1636. Providence was the second-largest city in New England, with a population of some fifty thousand. Hay quickly adapted to the city, the cultural and religious diversity of the students from all over the country and the high intellect of the faculty.

At Brown, Hay stood out mostly because of his dress. Unlike classmates from the eastern United States, his looks and appearance carried a "western" influence. But his intellect, wit, friendliness and love of humor (especially a good joke) made him an instant favorite among his peers. He was called "Johnny" by his intimate friends. But they also noticed something else about their friend's nature: his bouts with depression. Periods of melancholy would haunt Hay for the remainder of his life.

In the ensuing years, Hay studied Latin, Greek, mathematics, the classics (French and German) and sciences such as chemistry, physiology and geology. Political economics was also part of his curriculum, and according to school records, under Professor William Gammell, this is

Left: John Hay as he appeared during his days as a student at Brown University. *From* The Life of John Hay, *vol. I.*

Below: University Hall at Brown University. Hay's dormitory room was on the second floor to the right of the large tree. *Photo by the author.*

where he excelled. He also loved literature, especially poetry. Striving for success, his writing achievements earned him the reputation as the "best undergraduate writer in college." During the first terms at Brown, his busy schedule caused him to limit his extracurricular activities. In a letter home, Hay wrote, "I have no acquaintances out of the college; consequently, [I] know little of the city." Using his unique sense of humor, he closed the letter writing several postscripts, the last written as "P.P.P.P.P.P.S. That is all."

Students at Brown were required to memorize scores of passages from textbooks. A student related, "Hay put his book under his pillow and had the contents thereof absorbed and digested by morning, for he was never seen [doing anything] that could be construed into hard study." Today, he might be considered a man with a photographic memory.

As the college years flew by, Hay, like so many of his peers, admired pretty girls, perhaps at a distance until he mustered the courage to approach them. He also pledged to a fraternity, became the vice-president of a literary society and served as editor of the *Brown Paper*, an undergraduate journal. But his gift for poetry was never more apparent than when he read his own poem to an audience on Class Day, June 10, 1858. Described at the time as "a fertility of conception, a depth of sensibility, and a power of poetic expression," his words were rarely equaled at any future literary gathering.

But all good things must come to an end. That evening, Hay packed for home. The following day, he left for good—the wait for commencement exercises to be held that September seemed long, and his pining for home appeared too great. Hay would not return to Brown University again until 1897, when he received the honorary degree of Doctor of Laws.

After returning home, Hay was faced with a career choice. He was torn between finding employment in the literary field or the pursuit of law. He even thought about the ministry. Unable to make a timely decision, Hay again fell into melancholy. Part of his depression might have been the result of his transformation from a "westerner" to a gentleman of refined culture. In the end, he chose the legal profession. His Uncle Milton had a well-established practice in Springfield and welcomed his nephew into the firm. Next door was Abraham Lincoln's law office. They met mostly in passing but were familiar with each other. Lincoln, a former Whig, was now a Republican—"the party of the zealous young men in the North, who were resolved to prevent further encroachments by the Southern slaveocracy," Hay would write. The party ideas and platform appealed to young Hay, and he, too, joined the party.

John Nicolay, Hay's friend from their days together as students in Pittsfield, Massachusetts, operated a newspaper in Springfield. Lincoln enjoyed reading Nicolay's writings. When Lincoln made his run for the presidency, he wisely chose Nicolay as a secretary during the campaign, with Hay serving in the background. Shortly after Lincoln was elected, he appointed Nicolay as his private secretary. Soon Nicolay was inundated with secretarial duties far beyond what he initially envisioned. He needed help and knew just the man to lessen his load: John Hay. He approached Lincoln with the idea of bringing Hay to Washington, D.C. Lincoln's first response was classic: "We can't take all Illinois with us…" But after a pause, he relented: "Well, let Hay come."

The rest is history.

Part II

THE EXCITEMENT AND THE REALITY

DID SHE DESERVE THE TITLE "QUEEN OF AMERICA"?

Born in New York City in 1819, Julia Ward Howe was the daughter of successful Wall Street banker Samuel Ward, a puritanical Calvinist, and Julia Rush Cutler, a poet. Both of Julia's parents were well-to-do; she could claim Roger Williams, the founder of Rhode Island, and two governors from the state in her lineage. To say she was born with a silver spoon in her mouth is an understatement.

In the days when a woman's place was in the home, Julia had to struggle for an education. Growing up, she was bright and curious about all that was around her, and in the years that followed, much of what she learned was self-taught, although she did receive some private schooling. When her brother traveled to Europe and sent home a library of books, Julia read them extensively, all without her father's knowledge. When her father died in 1839, Julia and her two sisters moved in with her brother, Sam, who had recently married John Jacob Astor's favorite grandchild, Emily. Julia and her sisters benefited greatly from this arrangement, both socially and intellectually.

In April 1843, with both of her parents deceased, she accepted the proposal of physician Samuel Gridley Howe, a supporter of abolition, prison reform and better education for the blind. He was eighteen years older than his future spouse. Oddly, there was a time when Howe had shown more interest in Julia's sister Louisa than her—not the most opportune way of starting a marriage. The relationship was tumultuous from the start. Julia's husband was not much different than her father, as Howe kept Julia on a tight rein—something she regretted but learned to cope with in her early married years. Period accounts note that she suffered from depression because of her husband's inequitable treatment. But she was able to pull away from her husband's influence and begin her own career. However, marital troubles continued, and in 1852, they separated. Julia was soon living in Rome and her husband in Boston. Eventually they reconciled, but Julia became even more independent, and by 1876, when her husband died, Julia truly blossomed.

From the 1850s forward, Julia and her family lived in Boston, where she excelled both as a mother and as an intellectual. She traveled to Europe and Cuba and was able to develop friendships with Boston's elite—men like William Ellery Channing, Thomas Wentworth Higginson and Theodore Parker.

In 1853, the Howes maintained a summer residence in Portsmouth, Rhode Island, at the southernmost tip of the town near the Middletown border. The home at Lawton Valley was called Oak Glen. At the top of the hill on Union Street, less than a mile from her summer home, stood the Unitarian church where Julia preached and lectured. She would forever cherish her memories of living there. The home still stands today, not as a shrine but as a private residence.

When the Civil War commenced in 1861, Julia became a member of the U.S. Sanitation Commission, an organization determined to improve the health and sanitary conditions for soldiers in camp and on the battlefield. A year later, upon prompting by a friend to find more moving words to the tune "John Brown's Body," Julia published the poem "The Battle Hymn of the Republic," writing the lines while staying with her husband at the Willard Hotel in Washington, D.C., now called the "Crown Jewel of Pennsylvania Avenue." It was located only a block from the White House. This is how Julia remembered the episode:

> *I went to bed that night as usual, and slept, according to my wont, quite soundly. I awoke in the gray of the morning twilight; and as I lay waiting for the dawn, the long lines of the desired poem began to twine themselves in my mind. Having thought out all the stanzas, I said to myself, "I must get up and write these verses down, lest I fall asleep again and forget them." So, with a sudden effort, I sprang out of bed, and found in the dimness an old*

Music sheet for "The Battle Hymn of the Republic." Julia Ward Howe's poem first appeared in the *Atlantic Monthly*. *Library of Congress.*

stump of a pen which I remembered to have used the day before. I scrawled the verses almost without looking at the paper.

With poignant verses now associated with the original melody, the revised lyrics quickly became a definitive rallying cry for the Union. With the tumultuous reception the song received, Julia became an instant celebrity not only in America but abroad as well. Up to that point in her life, Julia had achieved mild acclaim writing books on poetry, drama and travel, as well as an abolitionist writer for her husband's newspaper, *The Commonwealth.* Now immensely famous, she was able to meet President Lincoln in Washington, D.C., and men and women like Edwin Booth, Lara Bridgeman, John Brown, Charlotte Cushman, Charles Dickens, Frederick Douglass, Henry Wadsworth Longfellow, Lucy Stone, Charles Sumner and Oscar Wilde.

Although her later writing never reached a parallel with the "The Battle Hymn of the Republic," Julia managed to succeed beyond measure with reform issues. In her lifetime, she championed such causes as women's suffrage, pacifism, world peace, prison reform, abolition of slavery, support for immigrants and education for women.

Julia had personality flaws that were very noticeable, and because of this, some detractors sarcastically dubbed her the "Queen of America." Period accounts indicate that she was vain and more than willing to voice her opinion about others. There are also indications of marital indiscretions—on whose part no one is certain. As a public figure, her vanity opened her up to all types of criticism. For a woman trying to circumvent the stereotypical views of her gender in the nineteenth century, she needed to exhibit tenacity and self-assurance more so than any man alive. Considering the times and her achievements, mocking her as "Queen of America" is most assuredly an undeserved title. In a newspaper tribute in honor of her eightieth birthday, a newspaper correspondent called her a "poet, preacher, [and] lecturer, champion of the oppressed of all nations, a loving mother and beautiful homemaker." The resounding tribute speaks for itself.

Maud Howe Elliot, one of Julia's daughters, once asked her, "Tell me, what is the ideal aim of life?" Julia paused but a moment before replying, "To learn, to teach, to serve, to enjoy!" Her life is a testament that she did all of these extremely well.

At the age of eighty-eight, she became the first woman elected to the American Academy of Arts and Letters. By the time Julia died of pneumonia on October 17, 1910, she had lived a rich and fulfilling life. Even after her

Julia Ward Howe as she appeared in her eighties. *Library of Congress.*

death, her legacy continued to be enhanced. In 1970, sixty-two years after her passing, she was posthumously inducted into the Songwriters Hall of Fame. A little more than three decades later, she was posthumously inducted into the Rhode Island Heritage Hall of Fame along with another state notable from her time: Major General Ambrose E. Burnside. Julia's remains lie at Mount Auburn Cemetery in Cambridge, Massachusetts.

The Rhode Island connection has left us some interesting artifacts from her life. A small room at the Portsmouth Historical Society (formerly the Unitarian church), located on the corner of East Main Road and Union Street, is dedicated in honor of Ms. Howe and is appropriately called the Julia Ward Howe Room. Within are a number of furnishings from Julia's Oak Glen summer residence, only a short distance down the hill on Union Street. An interesting item in the collection is a table used by Julia for writing. The table originally had tall legs, as Julia preferred to write standing. No one knows when, but the legs were shortened, perhaps to accommodate the exhibit. Also included in the collection is clothing that Julia wore when she lived at Oak Glen, along with a bedroom set and bedding. The building in which the collection is housed was added to the National Register of Historic Places in 1974.

THE GETTYSBURG GUN

Walking into the north vestibule of the Rhode Island Statehouse on Smith Street in Providence, visitors are immediately greeted by a capitol police officer standing near a metal detector/screening device. Although pleasant, the officer leaves no doubt that his assignment is all business. Be advised: if you never visited the Rhode Island Statehouse before, be prepared to pass through tight security. You will place all of your metal possessions in a plastic container and walk through the metal detector. Then, when directed, you will secure your belongings and walk away.

During the process, your attention may be diverted long enough to overlook some rather large and fascinating exhibits near the left and right walls of the white marble foyer. That's right. Even though the exhibits are sizable, processing through the security checkpoint is not only distracting but a bit unnerving as well. In your haste to gather your belongings, you may miss the brass James Rifle cannon. The artillery piece is parked diagonally to the right behind the screening device. On July 21, 1861, the cannon was engaged by Battery B, First Regiment Rhode Island Light Artillery, at the Battle of Bull Run. On the other side of the lobby, perhaps no more than twenty to thirty paces away, is a more fascinating exhibit: another cannon, but this one is rather special. This twelve-pound Napoleon saw significant action at the Battle of Gettysburg on the last day of fighting, July 3, 1863. The cannon was manned by the same battery as the one at Bull Run. Over the years, it has come to be known as the Gettysburg Gun.

There is something else that a visitor may miss when entering the statehouse. In glass display cases recessed in the marble wall near each cannon is a salute to our state's military past. Both cases contain the battle flags of Rhode Island regiments dating as far back as the Revolutionary War. Several are from Civil War regiments, such as the First Regiment Rhode Island Volunteer Infantry and the Fourteenth Regiment Rhode Island Heavy Artillery (Colored). All the exhibits display rips and tears from field use and normal age deterioration. As colorful and interesting as these flags are, the most fascinating display of all still remains the Gettysburg Gun.

Nearly every scholar of Civil War history knows about the cannon, although there are those who are still unfamiliar with the exact details. How was the cannon retired from service? Who were the men who sacrificed their lives while firing the gun, and how did they die? Where did the cannon reside after the war? And what precipitated its return to Rhode Island? Answers to these questions will be revealed shortly. But first, there is a caveat.

Armchair readers tend to forget or are unable to comprehend the gruesome nature of combat injuries. "Killed in action," "died heroically," "succumbed to wounds" or "mortally wounded" are the usual phrases used by authors, even eyewitnesses, to explain deaths during a military engagement. That is understandable. Sanitizing the nature of a soldier's death in battle provides a small measure of comfort, albeit temporary, to a family who sacrificed one of their own. But by protecting the emotions of a bereaved family, the scourge and devastation of war are unintentionally censored. When a person reads that at Antietam there were 22,717 casualties on a single day or that at Gettysburg approximately 51,000 were killed, wounded, missing or captured in three days of fighting, a general sense about the severity of the engagement is revealed. But war is about the art of killing and needs to be described in its deadliest sense. The dilemma of how best to describe battlefield deaths was touched on in an address given after the war to a graduating class at the Michigan Military Academy. The speaker was General William Tecumseh Sherman. His words resonate today just as they did some 150 years earlier:

You don't know the horrible aspects of war. I've been through two wars and I know. I've seen cities and homes in ashes. I've seen thousands of men lying on the ground, their dead faces looking up at the skies. I tell you, war is Hell!

Although not describing the specific incidents and the mangled bodies he witnessed on the field, General Sherman managed to convey the horrors in terms even a layman could understand.

The Gettysburg Gun and the soldiers who manned the piece contributed their fair share of destruction. The tale you are about to read is one that conjures the evil, cruelty and ruthlessness of war that General Sherman so succinctly described years later. The single most memorable incident relating to the Gettysburg Gun is savage, reported by a few who were there and managed to survive the ghastly affair. What these Rhode Islanders experienced was shocking and deeply personal. Their account of that fateful day was told if nothing more than to momentarily cleanse the body and soul—"momentarily" because incidents such as these are never thoroughly forgotten during a soldier's lifetime.

The story of Battery B and its cannons on the Gettysburg battlefield actually begins on the second day of July. By the end of that day, the battery had already suffered three killed, one taken prisoner and fifteen wounded. While withdrawing from the field, First Lieutenant T. Frederick Brown was wounded and had to relinquish his command to First Lieutenant William S. Perrin. Because the caissons and horses were left in the rear, the Confederates were unable to inflict any significant damage on them. Thus, the battery was well prepared for battle on July 3, with four cannons in full working order.

Waking the morning of the third after a call to arms, Battery B watched the sun rise over the horizon as the men listened to heavy gunfire in the distance near Culp's Hill. Not long after, the battery repositioned its cannons. Two middle guns were placed slightly in advance of those on the flanks. The morning passed uneventfully, although random Confederate artillery rounds destroyed several ammunition chests on the gun limbers. Sergeant John H. Rhodes best describes the next nerve-wracking hour:

> As the forenoon wore on, there came a lull, a stillness even of death. A feeling of oppression weighed upon all hearts, silence was ominous and portentous of coming evil. It was the calm which precedes the storm.

Suddenly, the silence was broken. The Confederates commenced firing, with cannon shot landing to the right of Battery B. This unholy barrage continued approximately every minute. Soon the entire Union line was ablaze with artillery fire. Battery B was ordered to its place. There the battery awaited orders to return fire. After ten to fifteen minutes, the men were given the command to commence firing. As Sergeant Rhodes explained, "It proved to be one of the most terrible artillery duels ever witnessed."

All the cannonading preceded one of the most well-known and documented events of the Civil War: Pickett's Charge. It was during this fiercely contested clash that one of the cannons from Battery B was struck by an enemy round, killing two men. Sergeant Rhodes explained:

> *The men were in the act of loading it. No 1, William Jones, had stepped to his place between the muzzle of the piece and wheel, right side, and had swabbed the gun and reversed sponge staff, which is also the rammer, and was waiting for the charge to be inserted by No.2. Alfred G. Gardner, No. 2, had stepped to his place between the muzzle of the piece and wheel, left side, facing inward to the rear, taking the ammunition from No. 5 over the wheel. He turned slightly to the left, and was in the act of inserting the charge into the piece when a shell from one of the enemy's guns, struck the face of the muzzle, left side of the bore and exploded. William Jones was killed instantly by being struck on the left side of his head by a fragment of the shell, which cut the top completely off. He fell with his head toward the enemy, and the sponge staff was thrown forward beyond him two or three yards.*

Alfred G. Gardner, the no. 2 man, suffered a devastating wound to his left shoulder, the enemy round nearly ripping his arm from its socket. Gardner, a pious man, was reported to have shouted, "Glory to God! I am happy! Hallelujah!" He died minutes later in the arms of Albert A. Straight, his sergeant and friend. Years later, when documenting the fierce encounter, Sergeant Straight described the confusion of the day thusly: "The rebels collected all their artillery and opened a concentrated fire upon us. It was terrible beyond description; the air was full of shell hissing and bursting. They came so thick and fast there was no dodging." Years later, Sergeant Straight would write that Alfred Gardner, who had been his tent mate on this campaign, requested that his Bible be sent home to his wife and to tell her that he died happy.

When the remaining soldiers attempted to reload the cannon, the twelve-pound iron ball became lodged firmly in the distorted muzzle. Numerous attempts were made to ramrod the round, all to no avail. Even after several blows with an axe, the cannonball could not be loaded or dislodged; half of the ball was jammed inside the muzzle, while the other half remained visible from the outside. As Sergeant Rhodes explained later, "as the piece cooled off the shot became fairly fixed in the bore of the gun." Since the piece was of no further use, Sergeant Straight was ordered to withdraw it from the field. By 3:00 p.m. the battery had been relieved and sent to the rear with its disabled cannon. Being in the rear, however, offered little relief. The battery still faced steady cannon fire the next few hours. Over two days of fighting, of the enlisted men in Battery B, five were killed, one was taken prisoner and another was reported missing. Thirty-two more were wounded, and two later died at a general hospital. Second Lieutenant Joseph S. Milne, on detached service from Battery A, Cushing's Fourth United States Artillery, was also mortally wounded and died within the week. The few men who were left unscathed from Battery B were temporarily assigned to Battery A of the same regiment.

After the battle, an ordnance team examined the gun with the cannonball stuck in the muzzle. Upon closer examination, the gun and gun carriage had been hit three times by solid shot or large shell fragments and an additional thirty-nine times by small arms fire. The gun was initially condemned to be scrapped, but a decision was made to retain it as a "curiosity of war," fit for a P.T. Barnum exhibit. Soon, the disabled weapon was sent to Washington Arsenal and eventually placed on display, where it remained until May 1874. Somewhere during that time, the cannon came to be known as the Gettysburg Gun.

In the early 1870s, Battery B held its first postwar reunion, and for several years after, the subject of the Gettysburg Gun drew intense and heated debate. Eventually, veterans of Battery B, citizens and politicians of Rhode Island, including the Honorable Henry B. Anthony, senator from the state, convinced Congress to grant Rhode Island sole custody of the piece. By act of Congress approved on February 19, 1874, and signed by President Ulysses S. Grant, the cannon was officially transferred to Rhode Island. Today, the transfer document is housed in the Rhode Island State Archives and is occasionally placed on exhibit in a glass display case. The document, written in scrolled text, appears more colorful and elaborate than the Magna Carta and still remains in pristine condition.

On May 21, 1874, a parade and demonstration officially accepting the gun took take place in Providence. But the early morning gray skies brought showers, with heavier downpours that continued into the afternoon. Because both military and veteran organizations had made the long trek from various ends of the state in the middle of the

The Gettysburg Gun at the Rhode Island Statehouse. In the background are regimental battle flags. *Photo by the author.*

afternoon, the order was given to assemble in spite of the inclement weather. Initially, a celebration had been planned in front of the Soldiers and Sailors Monument on Exchange Place, but the rain led to a change in the proceedings. The parade route was cut short, and the Music Hall was used for the exercise. The parade kicked off at 3:15 p.m. with a large contingent that consisted of nearly every veterans group from the state. Not long after the parade and ceremony, the veteran marchers came to be called the "Umbrella Brigade," for obvious reason. Only one month passed before the cannon would again be showcased at another parade in Providence on June 27.

For several years thereafter, the Gettysburg Gun was the featured piece at parades. For a time, the cannon was placed in front of the "Old Statehouse" on Benefit Street and later displayed in the foyer of a newspaper office in downtown Providence. Finally, in 1903, the cannon was placed in the Rhode Island Statehouse. End of story.

Well, not quite. For years, a number of people believed that the cannonball lodged in the muzzle was actually fired by a Confederate piece. Even today, many still adhere to that version as the true account of the Gettysburg Gun. Although it makes for good copy, the facts presented here are the accurate version of events that day. Then, in 1962, another incident took place.

Ninety-nine years, one month and twenty-one days after the cannon was removed from the Gettysburg battlefield, Dr. Wilfred E. Warren of Newport, Rhode Island, theorized that the gun could still be loaded with the original black gunpowder charge locked inside. After a 1908 affidavit surfaced from a member of the original gun crew (Private George Matteson) adding credence to Warren's theory, a decision was made to investigate further. On August 27, 1962, naval ordnance personnel and the Rhode Island National Guard successfully removed more than two pounds of black gunpowder after grounding and immersing it in water, then drilling out the touch hole in the gun barrel. Further examination of the gunpowder proved the substance to be highly volatile, a characteristic that occurs with aging. Technically, under apt conditions, the cannon could have exploded, inflicting untold injuries on unsuspecting bystanders.

The Gettysburg Gun now stands in the foyer of the Rhode Island Statehouse as a remembrance of a single episode in which heroic men from Rhode Island gave their all in defense of the Union. The men who fought at Gettysburg and all the other engagements of the Civil War have long since departed; the last, Albert Woolson of Minnesota, died in August 1956. In Rhode Island, John H. Riley, a veteran of Company H, Second Regiment, Rhode Island Volunteer Infantry, was the last surviving Grand Army of the Republic (GAR) member to pass away. He died on May 7, 1943. The stories of these veterans and their exploits now reside in history books, and the military equipment and ordnance they used—at least that which remains—now reside in special exhibits and collections throughout the country.

If possible, visit the Rhode Island Statehouse (only a short walk from the Providence Place Mall), see the cannons and battle flags, appreciate the message this exhibit conveys and salute those who helped preserve our nation, especially the brave young men from Rhode Island.

CASE NO. 721 TURNS INTO CASE NO. 428: PEREZ A. HOPKINS

Originally hailing from Yarmouth, Massachusetts, a maritime community made up of several small villages on scenic Cape Cod, Perez A. Hopkins, a likely descendant of Stephen Hopkins of the *Mayflower*, traveled a short distance west to the bustling city of Providence. Here he and his family settled in the Third Ward, an area with a large influx of immigrants. Textile manufacturing was booming in and around the region, and the chance to better his family's life had to be paramount in his decision-making. But living conditions would have been difficult. It was not uncommon in the 1850s for a family to live in one or two rooms of a rundown tenement building in the city.

Unfortunately, like many others during the mid-nineteenth century, he died at an early age: thirty-six. At the time of his passing, his son, also named Perez, was still a babe in swaddling clothes. Having to grow up in a city environment fraught with evils, temptations and other questionable distractions, and with only a mother to watch over him, it was not long before young Perez began testing the limits of the law. Eventually, his brushes with the police caught up to him. At thirteen, he was arrested, tried and convicted of theft. There was only one place in Rhode Island for an Oliver Twist–type delinquent like Perez: the Providence Reform School.

According to the school's register, now on file at the Providence City Archives, on December 29, 1858, under Case No. 721, a young vagrant of large stature named Perez A. Hopkins was remanded to the Providence Reform School by the Court of Magistrates. At first glance, it appears the punishment for theft may have been excessive, especially considering how many years Perez spent there, but placement in a reform school for adolescents committing petty crimes during the nineteenth century was not unprecedented and perhaps even fairly routine. As with all aspects of life during this period, times were tough; for all we know, Perez's mother, Charlotte, might have preferred her son's incarceration than face his incorrigible behavior on a daily basis. She died in 1861.

The Providence Reform School was established by an act of the Rhode Island General Assembly in 1850 after a petition by the Providence Association of Mechanics and Manufacturers, whose members were distressed over the high rate of juvenile delinquency in the city. In the 1800s, this problem manifested itself in every metropolis that experienced rapid and unchecked population growth as unskilled labor and destitute characters piled into cities with little more than the shirts on their backs. Many who came were either unable or unwilling to provide for their family's welfare. Some took to crime in an effort to put bread on the table. Providence was no exception.

A comprehensive search finally turned up a large building in the Fox Point section of the city to house the new institution for wayward children. Originally built in 1810, the structure was the former residence of General James B. Mason from the prestigious Brown family of Providence. More recently, the building had been used as a hotel. After purchasing the building, administrative personnel were selected to oversee the conversion and eventual operation of the school. The city mayor and six others chosen by the city council served as trustees. Their mission was to successfully implement three primary goals: "confinement, instruction and reformation of juvenile offenders and of young persons of idle, vile or vicious habits."

Before long, though, problems surfaced. It seemed that the administration was as incorrigible as the youthful inmates, as some rather devious and questionable activities were uncovered. In 1862, school administrators were accused of accepting bounties—more likely bribes—from recruiters to persuade young inmates to muster into the Union army to help quell the rebellion. Perez himself may have been coaxed into joining the service. An entry in the register on July 17, 1862, indicates that there were insufficient funds to continue with his confinement and that "an effort will be made to find something for him to do." Circumstantial evidence leads one to believe that Perez may have been unsuccessful earning his keep after working as a clerk under the school's work release program. Two days later, Perez A. Hopkins enlisted in Battery F of the First Regiment Rhode Island Light Artillery. Was this a coincidence? A rational person may think otherwise. Nothing has yet been found to prove anyone was prosecuted for accepting bounties at the school and exploiting the wards under the guise of patriotism.

Such irregularities may have been ongoing for years, but in 1868, a more serious scandal ensued. Both trustees of the school and the staff were accused of several wrongdoings: administering cruel punishments (flogging and beatings), changing children's names in an effort to conceal identities to parents, using foul and abusive language and misappropriating school property. The last charge stipulated that school administrators had confiscated Roman Catholic catechisms from inmates while forcing them to attend Protestant services. Undoubtedly, the tactic was employed in retaliation against those of Irish descent—the poor and destitute—who now lived in a country rife with immigrant stereotypes.

Carde de visite of Perez A. Hopkins. *Dr. Stephen Altic, DO, from his collection.*

As for the scandal of 1868, after lengthy hearings by the board of alderman, most charges proved inconclusive, although two supervisors were dismissed and some corrective action was taken. The questionable activities by the trustees and staff ultimately contributed to the institution's demise. In 1880, the State General Assembly assumed control of the facility—a bit late perhaps, but nonetheless, the die was cast. At the height of operation, the institution housed one hundred charges of both genders. With a seriously tarnished image, the school was closed, and the remaining boys and girls were transferred to two separate institutions: Sockanosset School for Boys and the Oaklawn School for Girls.

And what became of Perez A. Hopkins? Well, he did see war and quickly learned that his service was not as much of an adventure as was promised by the trustees of the reform school. On September 29, 1864, while serving with Battery F, First Regiment Rhode Island Light Artillery, Perez sustained shrapnel wounds from an exploding shell at Chaffin's Farm in Virginia. What remains unclear is whether he was wounded by a premature blast from his own cannon or by Rebel gunfire. During the battle, the battery experienced heavy Confederate resistance, which took down five men besides Perez: Michael Golden, James R. Price, Charles Whitman, James Wild and Henry C. Wilkie. Perez's wound proved severe, and his right forearm had to be amputated at a field hospital in the vicinity of the battlefield soon after the clash. The amputation was performed using the circular technique rather than the flap method. Although circular operations took longer to perform, the resultant stump was less prone to bleeding and infection and allowed soldiers to be transported greater distances. Perez was subsequently treated at several hospitals and eventually found his way to the U.S. Army General Hospital in Portsmouth Grove, Rhode Island, where he continued to convalesce before receiving a surgeon's disability discharge on May 22, 1865.

After his hospital release, Perez lived with his sister, Ann Elizabeth, and her husband, Thomas Waite, in Providence. Ann Elizabeth would only live five more years before dying at the age of thirty-two of consumption (today known as tuberculosis).

During the ensuing years, Perez had the dubious distinction of being mentioned by name and assigned a case number (428) in the highly comprehensive (or not the easiest of reads, as some would say) *Medical and Surgical History of the War of the Rebellion*. He was one of more than one thousand documented cases of men who experienced a primary amputation of the forearm due to shot injury in the war. The book acknowledges that of the cases examined for this particular surgery, there was a 9.6 percent mortality rate. Of further interest, the account noted that Perez's stump was "very tender" at the time of his discharge.

After his sister's death, Perez relocated to the state of Maine and became a farmer. There, in 1871, in the town of Somerville, he married Louisa A. Bram and fathered a child. He spent the next several years in and out of the Veterans Administration Hospital in Togus, Maine. The stress felt by his young bride, barely seventeen at the time, and his own physical limitations had to have caused many hardships. The marriage ended in divorce. In 1881, Perez married Mary Frances, the daughter of George Stearns, a former member of the Twenty-first Regiment, Maine Volunteer Infantry. Under this union, three children were born before Mary succumbed to an illness in 1887. Four years later, Perez married for a third time. His new spouse, Ellen Dolham, hailed from Jefferson, Maine. With her, he fathered four additional children.

In his youth, Perez was strikingly handsome, with light skin, blue eyes and brown hair. Keeping in mind that the average height of men during this era was about five feet, eight inches, Perez must have towered over many a man at six feet. After looking at his image, some might say that he seemed to possess an arrogant demeanor. More likely, the facial expression he wore that day for the photographer was nothing more than youthful self-assuredness and satisfaction in knowing that he now had a true purpose in life and, finally, a sense of belonging.

Long after the bugle call and drumbeats fell silent, and after years of toiling in the fields on a mortgaged farm as a disabled veteran, constantly caring for farm animals and, most importantly, providing for his large family, the strain became overwhelming. Adding to his woes were the long and harsh winters of Maine and, of course, the inevitable consequence of growing old. At the age of fifty-nine, another Civil War veteran was, quite possibly, ready to meet his maker. On November 7, 1904, Perez A. Hopkins died of a right pulmonary abscess. His remains are interred next to his second wife, Mary, at the James Preble (Whitefield) Cemetery in Lincoln County, Maine, on land situated east of Augusta. Perez's burial site is fitting, as those who have seen it say it is reminiscent of the countryside of Ireland, with burial stones telling of those who immigrated to this side of the ocean from the Emerald Isle.

Veterans Administration records reveal that Perez's third wife was still alive in 1951. Glenwood, one of their sons, served during the World War I era but never went overseas. Norman, the other son, also served in the military. Both inherited their father's blue eyes and stature. And like their father, they earned their status as armed forces veterans.

The Untimely Demise of Charles T. James

Born on September 15, 1805, in the small town of West Greenwich, Rhode Island, Charles Tillinghast James became a carpenter by trade and later an expert machinist and mechanical engineer. The technical disciplines that he acquired were largely self-taught. Rising swiftly in the manufacturing world and catching the eye of Samuel Slater, James is credited with establishing some twenty-three steam-powered cotton mills throughout New England as he offered his expertise on setting up manufacturing facilities and outfitting them with appropriate equipment and steam engines. Continuing on his amazing rise, he was elected a U.S. senator as a Democrat and served capably from 1851 to 1857. Soon he rose to the rank of major general in the Rhode Island State Militia. In this capacity, he took an interest in the design of ordnance.

Somewhere along life's journey, the town of West Greenwich proved too small for a gentleman of James's ability and ambition. The city of Providence seemed well suited and more strategically positioned for his manufacturing ventures. Here he settled in with his wife, Lucinda. While living in Providence, James accomplished some of his most innovative

Charles T. James, inventor. *John W. Melton Jr., LLC.*

work. On February 26, 1856, and June 10, 1862, the United States Patent Office granted C.T. James Letters Patent No. 14,315 and 35,521, respectively, for improvements to a cannon projectile. Called the Federal James Pattern Projectile, there were two versions of the shell: Pattern I and Pattern II. Both versions had their problems. Pattern I had a tendency to lose its sabot (lead ring) shortly after firing. This undesired result caused shrapnel to rain down on friendly troops immediately after the cannon was fired. Attempts were made to improve the design, but the Pattern II fared no better. It had two major problems: first, the shell caused excessive wear and tear to the rifling grooves, thus greatly diminishing the range and longevity of the cannon; second, the two-piece percussion either failed to explode or, when it did, the fragmentation was far less than desired.

Charles Tillinghast James was not to be deterred. On October 17, 1862, at Sag Harbor, Long Island, New York, he arranged for test firings of his projectile in front of foreign military officers. During the demonstration, one of the workers was attempting to remove a shell cap with pliers when it prematurely exploded. The worker was killed instantly, and James was mortally wounded. He died the following day. James was fifty-seven years old. His remains now lie at Swan Point Cemetery, Providence.

Today, historians still argue about which siege artillery round was more effective in the war. During the bombardment of Fort Pulaski, Georgia, both the James and Parrott projectiles (the latter designed by Robert P. Parrott) were fired, both with devastating results. The jury is still out as to which artillery projectile performed better.

Although major players, James and Parrott were only two of at least eight others during the Civil War who designed and manufactured countless renditions of cannon shells, looking for what Jack W. Melton Jr. described as the "search for the elusive, perfect projectile." In the case of Charles T. James, that search cost him his life.

A Chaplain's Duties

A paucity of information exists concerning the role of chaplains in the army during the Civil War. It is fortunate that Reverend Frederic Denison, AM, a chaplain with the First Regiment Rhode Island Cavalry and later the Third Regiment Rhode Island Heavy Artillery, left a written account about his experience during the rebellion. Hopefully, this short treatise fills some of the void.

Prior to the insurrection, Reverend Denison was a military man, serving initially as a private in the infantry and later as a chaplain. He drilled with the Pawtucket Light Guard of Pawtucket, Rhode Island, a city that bordered tiny Central Falls on the north and the sprawling metropolis of Providence to its south. Then the war broke out. Leaving his church in Central Falls, Reverend Denison joined the First Regiment Rhode Island Cavalry as a chaplain. From early 1862 until January 1863, Reverend Denison served with the cavalry unit in Maryland and Virginia. After suffering from exposure, he was transferred to the Department of the South, which comprised the states of South Carolina, Georgia and Florida. There he performed his chaplain duties with the Third Regiment Rhode Island Heavy Artillery until the unit was mustered out of service.

Army regulations were exceptionally vague as to the role of chaplains in military service other than to state that they were enrolled as staff officers and would hold the rank of captains. In reality, a chaplain's role was usually defined by the unit's commanding officer. A chaplain's main duties normally consisted of assisting surgeons, helping with hospital chores (taking care of the sick and wounded), ministering to religious concerns and conducting worship services. The chaplain also acted in several other capacities: as a mediator in disagreements between men; providing a shoulder to cry on for disconsolate soldiers; as a letter writer for the illiterate or those incapable of doing so; and, of all things, as a postmaster. For the most part, the chaplain moved with the staff, but when needed, he mingled with enlistees. Chaplains carried no weapons, generally wearing black suits without buttons that appeared a cross between a cleric and a military captain's uniform. In many ways, they were difficult to define in both mission and dress. Reverend Denison put it succinctly when he said, "There was no appointed or recognized place for him on a march, in a bivouac, or in a line of battle; he was a supernumerary, a kind of fifth wheel to a coach, being in place nowhere and out of place everywhere."

According to Reverend Denison, "During the war there were about two thousand volunteer chaplains serving about two million volunteer soldiers." The odds—one chaplain for every one thousand soldiers—were certainly not in the chaplain's favor. Without immense faith and unwavering tenacity, their message of comfort and faith would never have been so well received nor reached as many men. As Reverend Denison stated, "From large observation I can testify that soldiers have a high regard for devoted and faithful chaplains." Knowing that the men were far from saints, he added, "I know that soldiers, though often jocose and seemingly blunt in speech, have great tenderness of heart and are open to the highest hopes and aims of our imperishable natures."

When Colonel Alfred N. Duffie—a Frenchman whose hardest challenge appeared to be the English language—became commander of the Third Regiment Rhode Island Heavy Artillery, Reverend Denison was asked to serve as his aide. Duffie apparently had great difficulty stringing words together to write cohesive and meaningful messages. Reverend Denison accepted the challenge. Duffie was a Catholic and, according to Reverend Denison, had "very liberal views, caring more for 'the substance of doctrine' than for any particular forms and dogmas." Having high regard for religion, Duffie ordered that his men attend church services whenever possible on the Sabbath. Although services were unmistakably Christian, they were never "denominational or ecclesiastical" in nature. Once, a Catholic soldier asked to be excused from a service on the grounds that he was Catholic and Reverend Denison was a Protestant. Duffie's response was short and to the point: "You are a Catholic; very well; I am a Catholic; I attend services; I hear the chaplain; he does not hurt me; he will not hurt you; you are not excused; go to your place."

After the war, Reverend Denison returned to his civilian flock to continue performing many good deeds and apparently saving numerous souls throughout the state of Rhode Island. He also became a regimental historian for the First Regiment Rhode Island Cavalry. He died in 1901 at the ripe old age of eighty-two.

FINDING COMFORT FROM A MOTHER'S PRAYERS

The following narrative was abstracted from a book titled *Incidents Among Shot and Shell*, originally published in 1868 and written by Reverend Edward P. Smith, a field secretary of the U.S. Christian Commission (USCC). The book highlights numerous accounts recorded by the group during what the organization referred to as "the long years of the Civil War." The organization's primary mission was to save souls, but the USCC also provided social services and recreational activities to men in the army. In addition, members of the organization worked closely with the U.S. Sanitary Commission in providing medical services to the sick and wounded. One noteworthy incident in Reverend Smith's book concerned a Rhode Island soldier and is worth relaying in its entirety. The story was documented by Reverend Johnathon O. Barrows while in the field or shortly after the occurrence. Reverend Barrows, a delegate of the USCC, had spent a few days with the Eighteenth Regiment Maine Volunteer Infantry near Falmouth, Virginia, when he found the opportunity to visit a Rhode Island battery camped nearby. His account reads as follows:

> *I had noticed these artillerymen, as they galloped their horses each day, past my tent door to the brook below. So, one afternoon, filling my haversack, I paid them a visit. I found them ready to tell me much of hard fighting, deep mud, long marches and lonely days, but none could tell me of Jesus' love.*

This was very unusual; never before had I turned away from a company of men with so sad a heart. Suddenly someone called after me. It was a young soldier, and his first words, as he came up a little out of breath were—

"Do you belong to the Christian Commission?"

Almost before I could answer, he went on—

"I saw some of your men at Stoneman's the other day, and I got a book of them."

That was all the introduction; with trustful simplicity, he began to open to me the story of his heart:

> *"I was as hard as any of them when I came out, but I had a praying mother. It most broke her heart when I left home, for she knew I was wild and reckless. But she kept praying for me. Every letter she sent me, whatever else was said, she always told me that. But I didn't trouble myself much about it, till, one day, a letter came to me when we were in Poolesville. It wasn't very long, but it took a long time to read it, for mother was dead. I could see her after that, see the tears on her cheeks, and hear her say the old words, over and over again: 'I'm praying for you.' All through the Peninsula, it was still the same; she was right before my eyes continually. But I didn't give in till I came to Fair Oaks. I had worked hard all day at our gun; and when the firing stopped, I sat down on a log by the road, alone. They were taking away the dead and wounded near me. I thought how I had been preserved; and then the question came, 'What has God spared me for?' and then another, 'Had my mother's prayers anything to do with it?' They were solemn questions, Chaplain. Across the road there was sitting the only Christian in our battery. He saw I was thinking seriously; so he came over and asked me what it was. I told him. He was quiet for a little, then he asked me to go with him in a still place and pray. I went with him, and, on my knees, gave my heart to Jesus; you don't know how I love Him, Chaplain. My friend has been with me ever since; he's been a great comfort when the boys laughed; and ridicule isn't much anyways, if I can keep remembering how my mother's prayers save me."*

He led me to the friend who had prayed with him at Fair Oaks. Their hearts seemed knit together, like the heart of one man. But it was indeed "rivers in a dry place, and to a thirsty land streams of water," to find another to whom they could tell a little of their Christian fellowship. Tears came into their eyes and mine, as they told me how it seemed as if I must have come to the army especially to meet them, and to hear their story.

Somehow, as I went back to my tent, my sorrow and sighing had fled away.

Our Country Is Safe in the Hands of These Men

Shortly after the following story was told by a member of the Seventh Regiment New York Volunteer Infantry, who happened to be a witness to the event, it was published in the book *Christian Memorials of the War* by Gould and Lincoln in Boston in 1864. The tale was titled "They Ask God's Blessing":

While encamped in Maryland, I wandered off one day, and came to a farmhouse, where I saw a party of soldiers, who I supposed were Massachusetts boys, but who proved to be (though it is all the same) Rhode Islanders, who were talking with a woman who was greatly frightened. They tried in vain to quiet her apprehensions. They asked for food, and she cried, "Oh, take all I have, take everything, but spare my sick husband." "Oh," said one of the men, "we are not going to hurt you; we are nearly famished and want something to eat."

But the woman persisted in being frightened in spite of all efforts to reassure her, and hurried whatever food she had on the table. But when she saw this company stand about the table with bowed heads, and a tall, gaunt man raise his hand and invoke God's blessing on the bounties spread before them, the poor woman broke down with a fit of sobbing and crying. She had no longer any fears, but bade them wait, and in a few moments had coffee and other needed refreshments ready for them. She then emptied their canteens of the muddy water they contained, and filled them with coffee. Her astonishment increased when they insisted upon paying her.

The soldier witnessing the scene concluded his anecdote by saying, "Our country is safe, when such men go forth in the fear of God to fight for her."

THE VALOR OF GEORGE WHEATON COLE

The sloop of war USS *Iroquois* was launched at the New York Navy Yard on April 12, 1859, and was commissioned on November 24 of the same year. George Wheaton Cole, a gentleman from Providence, Rhode Island, served as a crewmember onboard the vessel. This is a story about Cole's final engagement.

George Wheaton Cole was born on June 1, 1840. Little is known about his early years; what is known is that Cole grew up to attend high school in Providence. From there, he entered the sophomore class at Dartmouth College in Hanover, New Hampshire, bypassing the freshman year. The start of the Civil War put a damper on many a young man's plans to further his college education, and Cole was no exception. As a patriot and an adventurer, he joined the navy on July 17, 1861, as a master mate. Shortly after, he received orders to join the crew of the USS *Iroquois*.

By early 1862, the USS *Iroquois* had become an integral part of the Mississippi River Squadron, in which the vessel performed blockade service near New Orleans, Louisiana. Its primary mission was to prevent blockade-runners from entering the harbor. But the squadron's ultimate objective was to capture New Orleans—the South's largest and wealthiest city—and Baton Rouge, the state capital.

On April 24, 1862, while taking part in an engagement below Forts Jackson and St. Philip, Cole was mortally wounded by a cannonball while serving as a gunner. The following is an eyewitness account of the heroic mate's final minutes:

> [Cole] *was engaged in superintending the men while loading a gun. A grape shot came through the side of the Iroquois while he was thus engaged, and cut him down. It passed through his body and almost cut him into two. As he reeled back and fell, some of the gun's crew quitted it and sprang towards him. Motioning them away, he partially raised himself, resting upon his right arm on the spot where he had fallen: "Boys, never mind me,"* he faintly [said].
>
> *"But you must be carried below, sir,"* replied one of the men.
>
> *"No! What is the use? I'm going. Look…look after the gun."*
>
> *He again fell back, and the men returned to their work. As he heard the report, he once again looked up.*
>
> *"Did it hit her?"*
>
> *"Yes, sir."*

The USS *Iroquois*. *From NavSource Naval History.*

The answer had fallen upon deafened ears. Scarcely had he shaped the
last question, [then] he had rolled backwards upon the deck, dead. Such
a death as this, is worthy of a niche in the memory of every true patriot.

Cole did not live to see the capture of New Orleans and the surrender to his
commander, J.S. Palmer, a few weeks later. Certainly his bravery on the twenty-
fourth played a contributing part in the successful undertaking of the mission.

During its service after the Civil War, the USS *Iroquois* led nine lives.
The sloop of war was decommissioned and recommissioned nine times
before being taken out of service for the final time on August 26, 1910.
Its record while in the service of the U.S. Navy was impeccable, no doubt
enhanced by the bravery of crewmembers like George Wheaton Cole.

DEATH PREMONITIONS

Nearly everyone knows about the poignant love letter that Major Sullivan
Ballou sent to his wife, the former Sarah Hart Shumway, back home in
Woonsocket, Rhode Island. If you have not read it, you more than likely
have heard a recitation of the words in Ken Burns's highly acclaimed
documentary, *The Civil War*. The letter is worth repeating in its entirety, as it
never seems to get old:

My very dear Sarah:

The indications are very strong that we shall move in a few days—perhaps tomorrow. Lest I should not be able to write you again, I feel impelled to write lines that may fall under your eye when I shall be no more.

Our movement may be one of a few days duration and full of pleasure—and it may be one of severe conflict and death to me. Not my will, but thine O God, be done. If it is necessary that I should fall on the battlefield for my country, I am ready. I have no misgivings about, or lack of confidence in, the cause in which I am engaged, and my courage does not halt or falter. I know how strongly American Civilization now leans upon the triumph of the Government, and how great a debt we owe to those who went before us through the blood and suffering of the Revolution. And I am willing—perfectly willing—to lay down all my joys in this life, to help maintain this Government, and to pay that debt.

But, my dear wife, when I know that with my own joys I lay down nearly all of yours, and replace them in this life with cares and sorrows— when, after having eaten for long years the bitter fruit of orphanage myself, I must offer it as their only sustenance to my dear little children—is it weak or dishonorable, while the banner of my purpose floats calmly and proudly in the breeze, that my unbounded love for you, my darling wife and children, should struggle in fierce, though useless, contest with my love of country?

I cannot describe to you my feelings on this calm summer night, when two thousand men are sleeping around me, many of them enjoying the last, perhaps, before that of death—and I, suspicious that Death is creeping behind me with his fatal dart, am communing with God, my country, and thee.

I have sought most closely and diligently, and often in my breast, for a wrong motive in thus hazarding the happiness of those I loved and I could not find one. A pure love of my country and of the principles have often advocated before the people and "the name of honor that I love more than I fear death" have called upon me, and I have obeyed.

Sarah, my love for you is deathless, it seems to bind me to you with mighty cables that nothing but Omnipotence could break; and yet my love of Country comes over me like a strong wind and bears me irresistibly on with all these chains to the battlefield.

The memories of the blissful moments I have spent with you come creeping over me, and I feel most gratified to God and to you that I have enjoyed them so long. And hard it is for me to give them up and burn to ashes the hopes of future years, when God willing, we might still have lived and loved together and seen our sons grow up to honorable manhood around us. I have, I know, but few and small claims upon Divine Providence, but something whispers to me—perhaps it is the wafted prayer of my little Edgar—that I shall return to my loved ones unharmed. If I do not, my dear Sarah, never forget how much I love you, and when my last breath escapes me on the battlefield, it will whisper your name.

Forgive my many faults, and the many pains I have caused you. How thoughtless and foolish I have oftentimes been! How gladly would I wash out with my tears every little spot upon your happiness, and struggle with all the misfortune of this world, to shield you and my children from harm. But I cannot. I must watch you from the spirit land and hover near you, while you buffet the storms with your precious little freight, and wait with sad patience till we meet to part no more.

But, O Sarah! If the dead can come back to this earth and flit unseen around those they loved, I shall always be near you; in the garish day and in the darkest night—amidst your happiest scenes and gloomiest hours—always, always; and if there be a soft breeze upon your cheek, it shall be my breath; or the cool air fans your throbbing temple, it shall be my spirit passing by.

Sarah, do not mourn me dead; think I am gone and wait for thee, for we shall meet again.

As for my little boys, they will grow as I have done, and never know a father's love and care. Little Willie is too young to remember me long, and my blue eyed Edgar will keep my frolics with him among the dimmest memories of his childhood. Sarah, I have unlimited confidence in your maternal care and your development of their characters. Tell my two mothers his and hers I call God's blessing upon them. O Sarah, I wait for you there! Come to me, and lead thither my children.

Sullivan

Sullivan Ballou's father died when he was four, leaving his mother, Emeline, the sole responsibility of caring for three children: Sullivan and his two sisters, Janette and Hannah. Scrimping every penny, Emeline managed to send Sullivan to prestigious Phillips Academy in Andover, Massachusetts, and then to Brown University in Providence. Eight years before the Civil War, Ballou became a lawyer after attending the National

Top: Major Sullivan Ballou, Second Regiment Rhode Island Volunteer Infantry. *From* Memoirs of Rhode Island Officers.

Left: Colonel John S. Slocum, Second Regiment Rhode Island Volunteer Infantry. *From* Memoirs of Rhode Island Officers.

Law School in Ballston, New York. In 1855, Ballou married Sarah Hunt Shumway. Soon they were blessed with two sons: Edgar and William. As a lawyer, Ballou became interested in public service. Not long after, he was elected to the Rhode Island House of Representatives on the Republican ticket, first serving as a clerk and later as the Speaker. When the war broke out, Ballou volunteered for military service and joined the Second Regiment Rhode Island Volunteer Infantry as an officer. His first battle—the Battle of Bull Run—was his last. He was thirty-two years old at the time of his demise.

Major Ballou died a valorous death shortly after mounting his horse and riding to the front in a vain attempt to better direct his men. Suddenly, a Confederate artillery round hit him in the right leg. His mount was killed instantaneously. Ballou was carried off the field, where his badly torn leg was amputated. Suffering terribly, he died and was buried near his colonel, John Slocum, near Sudley Church. The day ended with a resounding victory for the Confederates and an embarrassing loss for the Union.

Sometime after the Confederates abandoned the position, Union soldiers from Rhode Island were assigned the task of finding the burial site with the intent of bringing the remains of both men home. On the morning of March 21, 1862, the search party, aided by Privates Josiah Richardson, John Clark and T. Burgess, all of whom witnessed the initial burials, came upon the burial site. What they found was something they were not expecting: a disturbed grave. Nearby lay a soiled blanket with tufts of human hair that adhered to the fabric, along with charred remains of a femur, vertebrae and fragments of pelvic bone. Also catching their attention, two shirts were seen hanging from a nearby tree. Both shirts had Ballou's name and rank handwritten in ink on the collars.

A chilling tale from a young black female living in the area, later confirmed by another child and an adult, revealed that when the Confederates found the burial site of what they thought was Colonel John Slocum, they dug up the corpse, decapitated and desecrated what was left and burned the remains on the side of the riverbank. For reasons unknown, Ballou's personal belongings were hung in the tree, while the skull was taken by a Confederate soldier back home to Georgia, allegedly to be used as a punchbowl. Knowing that there were those who questioned whether the bone fragments found were actually those of the major, the soldiers dug up the remains in the adjacent grave that was left untouched by the Confederates. Within they found a decaying but still recognizable body. Looking at the face, they could see the telling sign of a distinctive red mustache. The remains were that of Colonel Slocum. Gathering

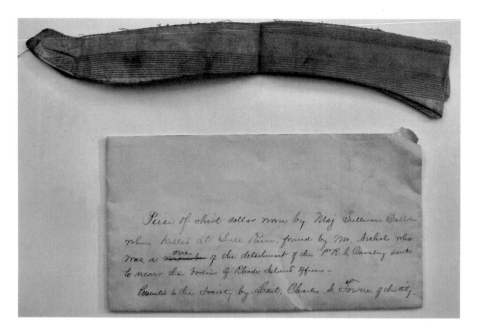

Fragment of soiled collar taken from a shirt found at Major Sullivan Ballou's burial site. Notice the faint signature on the right side of the fabric. *Providence Public Library, Special Collections.*

up the body of John Slocum and the remains and relics of Sullivan Ballou, the soldiers returned home.

Sullivan Ballou's remains were reinterred at Rhode Island's Swan Point Cemetery in Providence. Before the ceremony, one shirt was placed in Ballou's coffin, while the second shirt—the shirt Ballou was wearing on the day he was shot—was returned to Ballou's wife, Sarah.

Desecration of soldiers' bodies continued for the rest of the war, and the morbid practice was not confined to Southern soldiers alone. Arguably, there probably has never been a war in which dismemberments have not been perpetrated on bodies of deceased soldiers. The practice became a form of ghoulish celebration and retribution that resonated as a warning to the enemy that their turn would come.

Jumping ahead a century and a half later, in February 2009, a local historian stumbled on a noteworthy find at the Providence Public Library while looking through items in the Special Collections section. Hidden under a pile of books was a wooden crate that contained an assortment of documents. Written on the outside of one envelope were these words:

Piece of shirt collar worn by Maj. Sullivan Ballou when killed at Bull Run (and) found by Mr. Nichols who was one of the detachment(s) of the 1ˢᵗ R.I. Cavalry sent to recover the bodies of Rhode Island Officers. Presented to the Society [Rhode Island Soldiers and Sailors Society].

Within the envelope was the aforementioned relic. Most likely, Sarah Ballou donated the shirt to the society. As was the custom in the nineteenth century, relics were cut into smaller pieces and distributed as remembrances. Ballou's shirt must have experienced the same process. The collar band, with Ballou's name still visible, was given to Charles A. Towne, who in turn placed it inside the said envelope that was eventually rediscovered by the diligent detective work of a local historian.

As for the eloquent and now famous love letter, it was found in Ballou's trunk sometime after his death. Governor William Sprague of Rhode Island personally delivered the correspondence to Major Ballou's widow. Where the original copy of the letter now resides remains a mystery. Some feel it may have been buried with Sarah.

And what happened to Major Ballou's wife and children? Edgar, a graduate of Brown University (class of 1877), moved to Sierra Madre, California, where he owned a lemon grove. His brother, William, moved to East Orange, New Jersey. There he became a New York City food broker. Edgar passed away in 1924. William outlived Edgar by twenty-four years and is buried next to his parents at Swan Point Cemetery.

Sarah remained a widow. After the war, she was granted a widow's pension: twenty-nine dollars per month, which included a small sum for her children. After serving as a secretary for the Providence School Committee, she moved in with her son William, dying at his home on April 19, 1917, at the age of eighty-one. Sarah's remains lie next to her beloved husband. Whether she chose to have her husband's parting words inscribed on the grave memorial or it was the work of her children, the inscription remains for all visitors to read:

I wait for you there,
Come to me and lead
thither my children.

And what of the whereabouts of Sullivan's missing skull? According to a source who will remain anonymous, in 1993, he had heard that the skull was still in the possession of an elderly southern lady. "She's not very fond of Rhode Island," he said. Although the anecdote makes for good copy, who knows its validity?

The following account, written by Surgeon William James Burge, is his recollection of an incident that occurred on March 11, 1863. Although not related to the story here, it, too, concerns a death premonition. This story was told first-person to a Rhode Islander and is repeated here precisely as transcribed:

From the moment we came under fire at Port Hudson until we were out of range above six miles of continuous batteries, the Angel of Death and the Demon of Cruelty seemed to be in league for our destruction. It is impossible for one who has not had the actual experience of a naval encounter to conceive the awful sublimity of such a scene.

I had never before been under fire; and when the word came, on the morning of the eleventh of March, that we were to make the attempt to run the batteries that night, I anticipated the action with more curiosity than dread.

A young Frenchman of a fine appearance and amiable disposition filled the position of Captain's steward. His name was Charley Rich. He was a great favorite on board ship, and was allowed many exceptional privileges by the Commander, who fully appreciated him. During the afternoon previous to the engagement he closeted in a little store-room in the rear of the ward-room of which he had charge, as it contained the Captain's stores. In this room it was his habit to spend his leisure moments and occupy himself with books and in writing. At about sunset on this last day of his life he came from the room with a neat little package in his hand, and approaching me with the customary respectful salute he said: "Doctor, when you go down the river will you please give this to Louise?"

Somewhat surprised I replied. "Why Charley, aren't you going to stay with us?"

He smiled sadly and said, "I am sponger of the parrot-gun on the fore-castle and I shall be killed tonight."

I tried to laugh him out of so foolish a notion, telling him that I should be just as much exposed as he would and stood an equal chance of getting killed. His answer was, "Please take it, Doctor. I know this is my last day on earth."

At the little town of Plaquemine, down the river, there was a nice baker's shop, kept by an old Frenchman, and his three very handsome daughters. While patrolling the river we had frequently laid at anchor opposite this town for several days, together, and always took occasion to supply ourselves with fresh bread from the bakery, and not infrequently to refresh ourselves by a pleasant chat with one or other of the pretty girls who waited on us. Several of the officers, even, came near leaving their hearts in that little baker's shop, but Charley Rich, the Captain's steward, actually did it. He fell desperately in love with the youngest and most beautiful of the three girls, and his affection was fully reciprocated. Their chief opportunities for courting were during the young man's short morning call when he went for the Captain's daily supply of bread, and still they managed to obtain a peep into the condition of each other's hearts, and by the time we were ready to start on our perilous journey up the river they had plighted their troth, and were both looking forward to a joyful reunion in the near future.

I took the package from the young man's hand and locked it in my desk, making some mental reflection as I did so, about the stupidity of superstition and the utter absurdity of those who believe in presentiments or premonitions.

Just before midnight, at a moment when we were under the hottest fire and struggling past one of the principal batteries, I was sitting in the wardroom, which I had prepared for the reception of the wounded, and wondering who would be the first victim, when a hoarse voice called down the companionway.

"Doctor, here's a man with his arm shot off!"

"Bring him down quick!"

They laid him on the table, and as he was insensible I at first thought he had fainted from loss of blood, but on gently drawing the shattered arm away from the side I at once discovered that a large fragment of a bursting shell had passed through his body, and he was dead. I looked into the calm, pale face and recognized the Captain's steward, Charley Rich.

It was a great shock to me. No other man's death in that fearful conflict would have surprised me, but the literal fulfillment of a presentiment which I had so recently ridiculed filled me with a sense of the supernatural.

An examination of the package committed to my care, which was done by order of the Captain, revealed not only his devotion to his fiancée but also his positive conviction of the sad fate that awaited him. There was a daguerreotype of Louise, and a letter addressed to her, written in very good French, expressive of the most ardent affection. The closing portion of the letter was as follows: "Adieu, my beautiful darling Louise. I kiss you for the last time. I shall be killed tonight!"

On the glass which covered her picture was the unmistakable imprint of his loving lips.

Wm. J. Burge
Late A.A. Surgeon, U.S. Navy

He Died of What?

Albert L. Smith was born on July 16, 1822, in Thompson, Connecticut, a small town located on the south-central border of Massachusetts. Smith was a merchant by trade, but having the chance to defend his country, he enlisted as a lowly private in the Seventh Regiment Rhode Island Volunteer Infantry out of Pawtucket, Rhode Island. Recognized for his leadership abilities, Smith was promoted to first lieutenant on April 3, 1863, and eventually assigned to Company D. Slightly less than five months later, he died of brain fever at Nicholasville, Kentucky.

Five miles south of Nicholasville stood a four-thousand-acre Union supply depot. Known as Camp Nelson, the depot had the distinction of being the third-largest recruiting center for black contrabands (runaway slaves) during the war. There is a high probability that Lieutenant Smith had been assigned to this facility prior to his death.

But what exactly is "brain fever" (as it was called during the Civil War)? It is an inflammation of the brain, today known as meningitis. Whatever the name, the disease is debilitating. The scourge has two variants: viral and bacterial. Viral meningitis is less severe and can improve within days even without treatment. Bacterial meningitis, on the other hand, is life-threatening and requires immediate antibiotic treatment. Although there is no way of knowing, there is a high likelihood that Lieutenant Smith contracted the bacterial type and probably died in a matter of hours after initial exposure. His short illness probably included some and perhaps most of these symptoms: high fever, severe headache, stiff neck, vomiting, confusion, red ticks or skin blotches, cold hands, sore limbs and seizures. Although statistics vary depending on the source, it is fair to say that meningitis outbreaks during the Civil War accounted for between 8 and 10 percent of deaths by disease (dysentery was the most prolific killer, averaging between 45 and 50 percent of those who died of disease).

One fact is certain. Although swift, Smith's death was agonizing.

A Father's Misery: Mr. Walker's Reaction to the Loss of a Beloved Son

After two years of fighting with no end in sight, the war was taking a heavy toll not only on soldiers but also on those on the homefront as well.

In Newport, a merchant named Daniel Walker, an Englishman by birth, was despondent after losing a son at Antietam. The son had been serving with the Fourth Regiment Rhode Island Volunteer Infantry when he died. The remains were eventually brought home for burial. Unable to cope with the devastating loss, Walker committed suicide. The ghastly deed was accomplished in the gentlemen's privy, and his death did not come easily. After slitting his throat with a razor, Walker was still able to cause a scene by running around the yard, attracting the attention of the neighbors. Shortly after they came to his aid, he expired.

Later that morning, Coroner John W. Davis wasted little time in conducting an autopsy and summoning a jury for the inquest. Mr. Daniel Walker would become another forgotten victim of what Mrs. Mary Todd Lincoln called "that dreadful war."

Part III
THE WAR CONTINUES

In the Company of One

After spending nine months recovering from yellow fever at Lovell General Hospital in Portsmouth Grove, Rhode Island, Sergeant Charles Colvin of Company K, Seventh Regiment Rhode Island Volunteer Infantry, was issued a clean bill of health. In mid-June 1864, he returned to his unit in the field. But what he found upon his return was alarming. While he was convalescing in the North, the hard-fighting regiment—especially his company—had been decimated in battle. The following account tells the cruel tale.

Sergeant Colvin made his way through the line for daily rations. As was standard procedure, the sergeant presented himself by saying, "Here is Company K." The servers dishing out the provisions for that day were confused, at first; then they realized that Sergeant Covill was the only man alive or healthy enough from Company K to secure the provisions.

For Sergeant Covill and others in his company, it must have seemed that suddenly, the war had scoured the land like a violent tornado, taking a frightful and costly toll along its path.

THE LIFE OF THE
HONORABLE WILLIAM SPRAGUE

William Sprague was born in Cranston on September 11, 1830. His grandfather, also named William, was a manufacturer of cotton textiles and calico printer. In the early to mid-nineteenth century, the firm A&W Sprague Manufacturing was the largest calico printer in the world. Initially, the elder William established mills in Cranston and Johnston, but as the business prospered, he expanded the operation to smaller villages in the state. Every new site bordered a river that could generate sufficient waterpower to operate textile machinery. The other selection criterion was an immigrant population large enough to maintain a stable and affordable workforce.

As the business expanded, the Sprague family amassed huge profits—hundreds of thousands of dollars. In 1836, young William's grandfather died, leaving the manufacturing business to two of his sons: Amasa (young William's father) and William III (young William's uncle). Each son inherited an equal share in the business. Both continued with the expansion plans envisioned by their deceased father.

Amasa's son, William Sprague IV, attended "common schools" until he was sent to the Irving Institute at Tarrytown, New York, for two years. His education was cut short, however, after he received word that his father had been viciously attacked on December 31, 1843, and left to die in the snow (coincidently, the murder took place on young William's mother's birthday and his parents' wedding anniversary). The motive seemed obvious: retribution. Amasa Sprague had used his political influence to have a liquor license revoked that was issued to one of the Gordon brothers, owners of a pub near the factory. His employees were getting drunk at the pub during lunchtime and were incapable of performing satisfactorily at work for the remainder of the day. The subsequent trial of accused killer John Gordon, who was both Irish and Roman Catholic, was a seminal event in the state's judicial history. Although John Gordon was eventually convicted, two other brothers, Nicholas and William, were found innocent. With anti-Irish, anti–Roman Catholic and anti-immigrant sentiment running high, and a judicial system that acted as both trial judge and court of final appeal, John Gordon never had a chance. Although there were no witnesses and all the evidence was circumstantial, Gordon was led to the gallows at the state jail (now the site of a large indoor shopping mall in Providence) on February 14, 1845.

After Amasa's disturbing death, his brother, William, took control of the business and operated it with his son, Byron, and two of his nephews, one of whom was young William Sprague IV, who had been called back from his school in New York. Byron placed young William in the factory store and then the counting house. Here, young William learned the trade from the bottom up. His first assignments were menial tasks before progressing to more responsible duties such as bookkeeping and, later, as an active participant in the major operations of the business. When young William's uncle died in 1856, William assumed the leadership role in the business over his brother and cousin because of his ambition and intelligence.

But young William always had other interests in life. In 1846, at the tender age of twelve, he formed a company of young quasi-militia, and although he was the youngest of the lot, he was elected their leader. The year 1846 was a tumultuous time in Rhode Island. During the year, the state faced a major insurrection that came to be known as the "Dorr Rebellion." Although young William tried to play an active role with his militia, he and the group were shunned by state officials.

In 1848, at the age of eighteen, Sprague's real military career commenced when he joined the Providence Marine Corps of Artillery in Providence. Mustering in as a private, he quickly distinguished himself and was promoted to lieutenant and then captain. A few years later, his meteoric rise through the ranks elevated him to colonel of the entire company. Under his command, the company expanded to a full battery of artillery. Much of the success was due to Sprague's ability, but some can be attributed to his wealth.

In 1859, Sprague's health took a turn for the worse. As those with wealth usually did in the nineteenth century to mend their bodies, Sprague traveled to Europe to recover. After a seven-month stay, he returned in 1860 and found himself nominated as a conservative Democratic candidate for governor. Much of Sprague's popularity can be attributed to his family's name, his deep sense of patriotism and his affable personality. After a successful campaign, Sprague was not only elected but also became an ideal governor during a time of national unrest. Using his military experience along with an open wallet to raise, equip and subsidize a state militia at the outbreak of the Civil War, his unwavering patriotism, military acumen and financial generosity proved a godsend to the Union.

In February 1861, when things looked bleak for the nation, Sprague traveled to Washington and called on General Winfield Scott to make him

Top: Governor William Sprague IV. *From* Memoirs of Rhode Island Officers.

Left: Kate Chase, the belle of Washington, married William Sprague IV in an elaborate ceremony. *Library of Congress.*

aware of Rhode Island's military capabilities. Shortly thereafter, he made a similar offer to President Lincoln, following it up with a letter dated April 11, 1861, in which he reassured the president of the state's patriotism and its well-trained militia, which could be quickly mobilized to defend the capital against a Southern invasion. His letter also included a personal offer: "I am ready to accompany them," he stated in no uncertain terms. Perhaps more significant was Sprague's offer to donate $100,000 from his company's profits for use as desired by the Federal government and as the nation saw fit.

On April 15, 1861, along with all the other Union states, Rhode Island received President Lincoln's call for 75,000 men. As promised, it took Rhode Island only three days to send an infantry militia unit and a battery of light artillery (six guns and 150 men) to Washington. Two days later, under Colonel Ambrose E. Burnside, 600 infantry departed for Washington. Governor Sprague accompanied the men but later returned to enlist a second regiment of men under the command of Major John S. Slocum. Again, Sprague traveled to Washington with the men, this time staying at their side.

On July 21, the Rhode Island regiments along with the second battery of artillery suffered a resounding defeat at Bull Run. During the engagement, Sprague's horse was shot out from under him, and two bullet holes pierced his clothing without causing bodily injury. Because of his bravery, Sprague was commissioned a brigadier general; however, he was never mustered into active service.

After the devastating loss at Bull Run, Sprague returned home to raise additional regiments of men while serving as the governor. His services to the Union proved invaluable at a time when many Northern states had difficulty filling their quotas of men to fight the war. But his political status soon changed. He was elected to the U.S. Senate from Rhode Island for a six-year term that commenced on March 4, 1863.

By the end of 1863, Senator Sprague had married Kate Chase, the most desirable belle of Washington, who also happened to be the daughter of Secretary of the Treasury Salmon P. Chase. As a wedding gift, Sprague gave his beloved a diamond and pearl tiara said to be worth $50,000. After the marriage, Sprague maintained two households: one in Washington (Kate's father's estate) and the other in Narragansett, Rhode Island.

The first decade proved joyful for the Spragues, especially with the birth of their children: William ("Willie"), Ethel, Catherine ("Kitty," a special needs child) and Portia. In 1873, after the death of his father-in-law and a few years before leaving the Senate, Sprague's wealth began to decline. Other entrepreneurs, not only in the states but also overseas, lost money as well. The financial panic of 1873 and a nearly decade-long recession had taken a major toll on Sprague, monetarily and emotionally.

After leaving the Senate, Sprague concentrated on his manufacturing concerns, which were now spiraling out of control. He began drinking heavily and complained to acquaintances about Kate's extravagant spending habits in a time when frugality seemed essential. Many believed that Sprague had now become physically and verbally abusive to Kate, while additional failings in their relationship became more evident. There were also accusations that Kate was having an affair with New York senator Roscoe Conkling. Supposedly, in 1879, Sprague caught Conkling with his wife and chased him off his Narragansett estate. The affair ended, but the marriage appeared doomed. Three years later, the couple divorced.

Kate reclaimed her maiden name (Chase) and left for Washington to live with her daughters on her deceased father's estate. Adding more misery to the Sprague/Chase tragedy, their son Willie took his life at the age of twenty-five. The death shattered both parents, but Kate more so. With little or no alimony and her father's inheritance all but exhausted, Kate took up farming and raised chickens. She became a recluse, and in 1899, she died in poverty after suffering liver and kidney failure at the age of fifty-eight.

William Sprague fared somewhat better. After the divorce, he married Dora Inez Clavert of West Virginia in 1883 while continuing to delve into local politics in the town of Narragansett, Rhode Island. Then the unthinkable happened: Sprague's homestead burned to the ground in October 1909. In an effort to save his diaries and other artifacts collected over his lifetime, Sprague rushed into the house but was overcome by smoke and had to be revived. Although his life was spared, all of his personal possessions were lost.

After the devastating fire, the couple decided that a move to Paris was appropriate. Six years later, on September 11, 1915, Sprague died of meningitis, a day short of what would have been his eighty-fifth birthday. His body was returned to Rhode Island and interred with full military honors at Swan Point Cemetery in Providence. Sprague was the last U.S. senator to pass away who had served during the Civil War.

A DAY OF RECKONING WITH THE "CONFEDERATE AIR FORCE"

While preparing to evacuate Harrison's Landing during the Peninsula Campaign, Sergeant John H. Rhodes, a member of Battery B, First Rhode Island Light Artillery, experienced a troubling encounter with the "Confederate Air Force" headquartered in Virginia. He was standing in an old mansion that happened to be the birthplace of President William Henry Harrison. During the evacuation, it was being used as a hospital. In the granary on the plantation was an embalming house, occupied by a Dr. Holmes of Brooklyn, New York. Here is how Sergeant Rhodes told the story:

> At this season of the year the surrounding country afforded an interesting field for the enthusiastic amateur or professional entomologist. Every creeping thing that Noah permitted to enter the ark, and some, perhaps, that he did not, were to be found here. Some specimens being decidedly ill-favored, and by no means desirable as companions. Talk of "rats in Brazil," or "cockroaches in Japan," they were not a circumstance to the fly tribe at Harrison's Landing…Remember, the mercury was at 100 degrees and sometimes reaching 110 degrees in the shade; you "strike the air" with a quick, irregular motion of the hand, hoping to catch your tormentors, but they only increase their zealous attacks for this attempt at self-defense. Buzz! Buzz! Buzz! Flies on the nose; flies in the ears; flies in the food; flies in the tent; flies in the air outside; you attempt a short nap, flies take possession of you, and it is a failure; black, biting, merciless flies everywhere.

Not only were the Union men uncomfortable from the ever-persistent squadron of dive bombers, the horses were, too. As nerve wracking as it was for the soldiers, so it was for the horses. Unfortunately, there was little the animals could do to ward off the pesky air attacks, although they tried in numerous ways: shaking their heads, lifting a leg while scratching the other, snorting, jumping in place, fanning their tails and localized body twitching.

Left unsaid but what was obviously on Sergeant Rhodes's mind was the location of the embalming house, which must have played a major role in attracting the menacing creatures from the southern sky. Sergeant Rhodes concluded his narrative by saying, "In a fair fight the rebels can be vanquished, but flies in fly-time—never! No, never!!"

RHODE ISLAND'S TIES TO THE BATTLE OF FREDERICKSBURG

Rhode Island maintains two connections to the Fredericksburg, Virginia battlefield. The first is well known and has to do with a major player in the event. The second is a modern, more remote association that pays tribute to an act of bravery performed on December 13, 1862.

The first Fredericksburg connection involves the Union commander at Fredericksburg, Major General Ambrose E. Burnside. Born in Liberty, Indiana, Burnside moved to Bristol, Rhode Island, where in 1853 he set up residency and opened the Bristol Firearms Company to produce his invention, a magazine-fed breech-loading rifle called the Burnside carbine. (The company went bankrupt in 1860 but continued to manufacture weapons for the military under the ownership of his creditors.) Burnside lacked General George B. McClellan's huge ego. When given command of the Army of the Potomac by President Lincoln, Burnside felt unqualified for the honor. In fact, he had turned down two previous promotions. This time, Burnside felt obligated to accept as he was "ordered" and not "asked" to assume command. With reluctance, he accepted the enormous task at hand.

Although this chapter is not the place to recount the Battle of Fredericksburg proper, it is important to understand a few specifics about what transpired there. As the new commander, Burnside developed a plan to use the Army of the Potomac to capture the Confederate capital of Richmond. The route south would take his army through Fredericksburg. The campaign commenced on December 11, 1862, and lasted until December 15, 1862. But luck was not in his favor. Between bad weather, poor topographical maps and a lack of pontoon boats needed by his army to cross the Rappahannock, getting his men to and through Fredericksburg proved a nightmare.

The real debacle, though, took place on the thirteenth, a cold and overcast day, and it was something Rhode Islanders preferred to forget. On that date, Burnside launched wave after wave of frontal assaults on a Confederate line positioned behind a stone wall on top of a hill, a near-impenetrable position known as Marye's Heights. Union men died en masse. Witnessing the slaughter from a nearby command post, General Robert E. Lee said, "It is well that war is so terrible or we should grow too fond of it." Lee later commented that the Union assaults on Marye's Heights that day were "utterly hopeless." History records that fourteen frontal assaults were

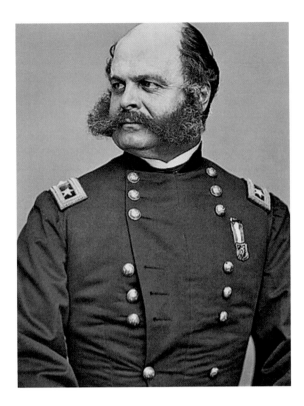

Major General Ambrose E. Burnside, pictured here with his famous whiskers. *Library of Congress.*

attempted to take the hill, yet not a single unit breached the Confederate position. By the end of the day, when darkness settled in, the Union army suffered seven to eight times more casualties than the Confederates.

The Union army was soundly defeated. Burnside blamed his subordinate generals for the failure; the subordinates blamed Burnside. Six weeks later, President Lincoln removed Burnside from command. In 1864, like the phoenix, Burnside rose again during the Siege of Petersburg only to direct another massive misadventure that came to be called the Battle of the Crater. At this clash, the Union lost 504 killed, 1,881 wounded and 1,413 missing or captured. Later, a court of inquiry censured Burnside for his failure of command and relieved him of all further duties.

The second connection to Fredericksburg involves a monument placed close to the battlefield more than a century later. The story begins on the night of the thirteenth, after the assaults had ceased. The cries of a multitude of Union casualties lying unprotected on open ground echoed in the wind. A nineteen-year-old Confederate, Richard Rowland Kirkland, already a hardened combat veteran from Flat Rock, South Carolina, serving with Company E, Second Regiment South Carolina Infantry, heard the wretched cries of the Union casualties and was moved by their suffering and unrelenting pleas for help. Because the field of carnage was a no-man's-land where a soldier from either side could be shot by a sniper while performing the simple act of raising his head, no one dared to comfort the wounded. The only exceptions were those fortunate enough to remove themselves from the field under their own power while praying they were not on the receiving end of a bullet. The more seriously injured were left to die.

By the morning of the fourteenth, the cries of the wounded had yet to subside. The haunting pleas for food, water, blankets or medical assistance fell on deaf ears. Although no one was willing to risk life and limb in the face of certain danger, Kirkland could stand it no longer and asked permission of his commander to help the Union wounded. After first denying the request, General Joseph Kershaw gave Kirkland his consent. Gathering all the canteens he could find and filling them at a nearby well, Kirkland raced up the hill, assisting as many wounded as he could in the little time he had. Some accounts state that General Kershaw watched as Kirkland performed his mission of mercy that continued for more than an hour. Union soldiers witnessing the heroic feat withheld fire. Kirkland performed his humanitarian act not once but numerous times, running back and forth to fill canteens and then returning to the field to provide aid.

Kirkland went on to fight in other major battles like Chancellorsville and Gettysburg. At the Battle of Chickamauga, Kirkland was mortally wounded by gunshot. His final words were, "Tell my pa, I died right."

Decades elapsed before Kirkland's bravery was honored. Dr. Richard Lanier, a dentist from Fredericksburg and director of the Fredericksburg Centennial Commission, persuaded the South Carolina and Virginia legislatures to assist with the funding effort. The Richard Rowland Kirkland Memorial Foundation, as it was called, also included Kirkland's descendants. The fundraising effort proved a resounding success. A monument was designed and eventually erected near the battlefield on land owned by Mary Washington College to serve as a tribute to a soldier's compassion for his fellow man regardless of which side he fought. The official dedication ceremony took place on September 29, 1965. In 1987, the land was deeded to the National Park Service.

But where is the Rhode Island connection? The Richard Rowland Kirkland statue was sculpted by the world-renowned master Felix de Weldon, then a resident of Newport, Rhode Island. He and his wife and

This monument was erected in memory of the heroic acts of Richard Rowland Kirkland on the Fredericksburg battlefield. *Peter Ducas.*

children lived on a twelve-acre estate called Beacon Rock on the shores of Narragansett Bay. De Weldon is best known for the majestic Marine Corps War Memorial (also called the Iwo Jima Memorial) in Arlington, Virginia, along with a host of other historic sculptures, said to number about 1,200, that are scattered throughout the world. In 1996, De Weldon lost his home and much of his assets due to financial hardship. He died on June 2, 2003, at the age of ninety-six in Woodstock, Virginia.

Now an interesting sidelight: a historian recently questioned whether Richard Rowland Kirkland actually performed the valorous deeds credited to him. Was the story a parable to enhance Southern chivalry after the war, or did Kirkland actually perform those deeds? Due to the lack of eyewitness accounts and the fact that Kirkland's deeds were never mentioned in after-battle reports by those who were there, especially General Joseph Kershaw's description of the battle, there remains an iota of doubt that the events as described actually transpired.

Responding to the possibility that the Kirkland story was a myth, one gentleman said, "Skepticism about the Kirkland story is reasonable...but before dismissing Kershaw's account...[the historian] needs to persuade us that Kershaw is an unreliable witness." A South Carolina resident put it bluntly: "You can believe your tale, we know ours."

In defense of the story and the lack of any mention of Kirkland's bravery in after-battle reports, a reasonable answer may be: why would there be? What Kirkland supposedly braved was far outweighed by the battle, tactics, successes and the extreme carnage witnessed that day. Acts of compassion, especially helping the enemy, were rarely mentioned, if ever, in after-battle reports.

Richard Rowland Kirkland is a hero. If nothing less, he gave his life to "the cause." His entire service record has earned him the right to have his memory honored and, more importantly, to rest in peace.

A BAWDY LETTER

Camp followers—a less offensive phrase used to label common prostitutes—were as available to soldiers as stale hardtack, spoiled meat and bad whiskey. Wherever soldiers traveled, women of ill repute were sure to follow. Several sources tell of camp followers overrunning entire towns to ply their trade after men returned from the field. One perceptive soldier in a letter home to his wife expressed the view "that one house in every ten is a bawdy house." Public women—another phrase associated with these ladies of the evening—were so common around Washington, D.C., and Alexandria, Virginia, that by 1864, 525 brothels were open for business, employing approximately 7,500 loose and lascivious ladies.

Prostitution became a large and profitable enterprise during the war. Neither Union nor Confederate soldiers were exempt from its temptations, as both sides were served by the trade—a welcome diversion for many. On the downside, prostitution brought a greater risk of contracting sexually transmitted diseases. Syphilis and gonorrhea were fairly widespread, especially in larger cities, causing civic leaders to find ways to curtail the profession. In the end, they had little success in shutting down the industry.

Although many soldiers refused to partake in such extracurricular activities, there were thousands more who did. As could be expected, a majority remained silent about their sexual escapades for fear of embarrassment should their families find out about their indiscretions. Yet, and perhaps not surprisingly, there were those who told of their adventures with manly bravado in letters home to their friends. For obvious reasons, few of these letters have survived. One such letter that did, however, was written by an enlisted soldier from an artillery outfit: Battery D, First Regiment Rhode Island Light Artillery.

In the initial paragraph of a letter dated January 14, 1862, written at Camp DuPont and mailed to a friend back in Rhode Island, we learn that our soldier had been recently thrown from a caisson, hurting both feet and a knee. Although still smarting from the injury, he wrote, "I can fight if I get a chance," and that he is "not sick of a soldier's life yet." He also talked about the unpredictable Virginia weather in January and some of his friends who also experienced similar trials and tribulations with noncombatant injuries. After dispensing with the typical formalities so reminiscent of thousands of other soldier's letters of the time, he tackled the subject at hand. "We feel pretty stiff," he said, referring to himself and one of his friends. "We would like to get limbered up. Woman are scarce here, mostly black at that. Smoke meat is good but we would like to have a change," using the derogatory description to refer to black female contraband. He went on to state that his friend Jeremiah D. Hopkins will not have sex with these women and quoted him as saying that "he ain't touched anything since he came from home." Apparently, Jeremiah had been smitten by a gal back home named Emily Austin, and until he returned from the war and tried his luck with this fair lady, he was determined to remain chaste. In 1862, Emily would have been about eighteen years old and still residing with her parents and two siblings.

In the following paragraph of the letter, the soldier bragged about sleeping with his friend—a nonsexual practice common during the era—and wrote tongue-and-cheek about sodomizing him by using a vulgar term, although it appears he is only joking. We may never know for sure, though, as homosexuality was not uncommon in either the Union or Confederate army.

Continuing his lascivious letter, he told about a friend in the field who was onboard a vessel where several loose women were plying their trade. Whether his friend took advantage of the opportunity is not explained, but there is every indication that the writer of the letter wished he was present at the time.

In one of the closing sentences, our adventurous lad asked his friend to "write all about the girls" back home while in the same breath telling him

Gallant veterans. *From* Battery D, First Rhode Island Light Artillery in the Civil War, 1861–1865.

not to show this letter to anyone. In return for his secrecy, he promised to "write…a better one next time."

Not to be outdone by his imprudence, at the end of the letter, the Rhode Island soldier drew a rudimentary image of a female sex organ, writing the anatomical slang name and adding the words, "black at that." In addition, he instructed his friend to "tell the girls [I] will come home and sponge their pieces one of these days."

The lad from Battery D, First Regiment Rhode Island Light Artillery, did not survive the war. He died far from home before getting the opportunity to prove his sexual prowess to the girls back home. Two of the friends he mentioned in the letter survived and lived to be photographed at a veterans association gathering held at Roger Williams Park in June 1891. Neither man—John S. Gorton or Jeremiah J. Hopkins, who had been seriously wounded in his left leg by a bullet at Antietam—was implicated for sexual indiscretions in the aforementioned letter. As for Emily Austin, we may never know whom she married, and that is a pity. Whether Jeremiah courted Emily after his early discharge in 1862 due to the seriousness of his wound is unknown. What we do know is recorded in the 1870 U.S. Census. Jeremiah returned to his profession as a farmer and married a lady named Eunice Ann. He lived a long life, dying at the age of 101 in 1941. Jeremiah was one of the last surviving Civil War veterans from the state (his photograph is included in a later story).

HARPER'S WEEKLY ILLUSTRATOR
JOHN REUBEN CHAPIN

During the Civil War, the primary source of information was newspapers. Although biased and opinionated, daily newspapers were a basic necessity for nearly everyone. With steamship and railroad arrival and departure schedules; high and low tide forecasts; political and financial affairs analysis; editorial comments (swayed by party allegiance); local, national and international news coverage; and, most importantly, war coverage, newspapers were a daily staple.

Just as today, a large percentage of print space was reserved for product and service advertisements, which offset publication costs and generated large profits in return. Most notable were advertisements for medical treatments and cures, the majority having no therapeutic value. A plethora of claims by bogus doctors were not only fraudulent but also outright deadly. Still, newspapers were a hot commodity, as any news (no matter how suspect) seemed better than no news.

Competing with daily newspapers during the war were weekly publications such as *Harper's Weekly* and *Frank Leslie's Illustrated Newspaper*, to name the two largest. Not only did they provide readers with a supplement to daily newspapers, but they were also filled with illustrations and editorial cartoons—a welcome respite for many who had to rely on their vivid imaginations. Both publications got their start by emulating the well-established and hugely successful *Illustrated London News*. These weekly newspapers became the forerunners of today's modern news magazines.

Based in New York City, *Harper's Weekly* in 1860 claimed a circulation of 200,000, nearly three times that of its closest rival, *Frank Leslie's Illustrated Newspaper*. *Harper's* started as a monthly edition in 1850 (*Harper's Monthly*). By 1857, *Harper's* had introduced a weekly edition and changed its name accordingly. Although *Leslie's* was the first to appear on newsstands as a weekly in 1852, the newspaper seemed to be no match for *Harper's* commitment to hiring high-quality illustrators like Winslow Homer, Granville Perkins and Livingston Hopkins. Further increasing its foothold in the publishing realm, *Harper's* included political cartoons by wildly popular Thomas Nast along with timely and detailed news coverage about the war. If there was a single valid criticism about the publication, it concerned its moderate view regarding slavery. *Harper's Weekly* middle-of-the-road approach to the evils of slavery earned it the nickname "*Harper's Weakly*." But in the end, what

A sketch by John Reuben Chapin. *Dr. Stephen Altic, DO, from his collection.*

gained readership respect was its superiority in reporting the war over all other competitors. The better-quality illustrations also put it at an advantage at a time when newspapers lacked the technology to print photographs.

There were also lesser-known illustrators who worked for Harper's either as employees or contributors during the war. Men like Theodore R. Davis, Henry Mosler and the brothers Alfred and William Waud. Then there was John Reuben Chapin. Today, Chapin is a virtual unknown, yet his work for *Harper's Weekly* was instrumental to the periodical's success. Although a talented wood engraver, illustrator and watercolorist, Chapin was hired by the journal to organize and supervise the Art Department, which he did successfully for years. While there, he also developed the block engraving process that aided in the production of woodcuts. Wearing several hats, Chapin is also credited with writing articles while in its employ.

John R. Chapin was born in Providence, where he lived comfortably during his youth. Records indicate that Chapin moved out of Rhode Island in the 1830s. His mother, Emaline Amelia Thurber, a learned woman, was a member of a prominent family from the city. (Anyone who knows or travels the main interstate through Providence cannot help but notice the large Department of Transportation sign for the famous—some say infamous—Thurber's Avenue, referred to by locals as the "Thurber's

Avenue curve.") Emaline's husband, Loring Dudley Chapin, was originally from Springfield, Massachusetts, but moved to Providence in 1818. Here the elder Chapin manufactured musical instruments and is credited with opening the city's first music store. By the 1830s, the entire Chapin family had moved to New York City, where young John attended "Normal School." Here Chapin honed his skills as an illustrator. He was fortunate to have a father who loved books containing numerous illustrations; John studied them to enhance his skills as an artist. Urged by family friend Samuel F.B. Morse (the later inventor of the telegraph), Chapin attended the Academy of Design in the city, where Morse served as an arts professor.

At the age of nineteen, Chapin received an appointment to the U.S. Military Academy at West Point but never pursued the opportunity. Rather, he became a law clerk. Chapin lasted but six months in his new profession before setting off for Boston to follow his artistic dream.

At the age of twenty-five, Chapin married Martha Carson Shannon, a former Providence resident, in August 1848. For the next decade, Chapin worked in New York City as a freelance artist for books and magazines, as well as at the patent office in Washington, where he drew patent sketches for successful inventors—men like Cyrus McCormack (the reaper) and Walter Hunt (the Springfield rifle). Six years later, the family settled in Rahway, New Jersey. By now, Chapin had become relatively prosperous, as evidenced by his employment of seven black servants to help his wife raise their children. In 1863, and now nearly forty, Chapin became captain of Chapin's Battery, a New Jersey Militia unit. With the war raging, Chapin illustrated several Alfred Waud rough sketches sent to him from the battlefield for *Harper's Weekly*.

In about 1870, along with his wife and five children, Chapin moved to Buffalo and opened his own company called the Bureau of Illustration, hiring several illustrators to support the needs of various Buffalo businesses. Chapin's move to Buffalo was short-lived, but in 1890, after working in Chicago, New York and Boston, he and his wife returned to Buffalo. This time, they resided with one of their sons. From the household, Chapin freelanced as an illustrator and watercolorist until his passing in 1904. There is no indication that Chapin ever set foot in Providence again after leaving for better opportunities elsewhere.

Harper's Weekly, where Chapin's artistic talents were first admired by multitudes, closed shop in 1916. *Frank Lesley's Illustrated Newspaper* folded six years later.

Just One Apple

The following tale was told by a member of Battery B, First Regiment Rhode Island Light Artillery, and was published in the battery regimental history.

As the men in Battery B were making their morning pot of coffee, a train rolled in with a number of wounded Union soldiers from Second Bull Run. Many asked for water or coffee. The men of Battery B were happy to oblige, not only filling the canteens of the wounded but also giving them slices of melons that were recently stolen from a sloop by a corporal of the battery.

In the meantime, a sutler boarded the train to sell his apples. Seeing the peddler, a famished drummer boy who lost an arm at Second Bull Run begged for an apple. The sutler responded, "I sell my apples, I don't give them away."

Overhearing the conversation, a battery man replied, "Oh give the poor boy one."

"Not by a damned sight," the sutler said.

As the original storyteller related the tale: "*Then something happened*, and the peddler sat down in a most unexpected manner; the basket of apples changed hands, and drummer boy had more than one apple."

Assuming the battery man was right handed, the *something that happened* most likely was a strategically directed hard right cross.

Kady Southwell Brownell

Several substantiated accounts tell of women posing as men while fighting to preserve the Union. Photographic images that survive today show them wearing homemade uniforms and brandishing weapons. These remarkable ladies—some say as many as 250—managed to remain undetected, not simply for weeks but years, before their elaborate masquerade unraveled. In one case, the gender of a female fighting as a male was identified only after she suffered serious battlefield wounds that required treatment at an army field hospital. Imagine the astonishment of the doctor, thinking that he was operating on Private John Doe and realizing that the patient was Private Jane Doe. But Rhode Island can top this story: a young woman named Kady Southwell Brownell openly served as a woman in the Union army, although questions remain as to the extent of her heroism and her official status as a soldier.

The year was 1842. In an army camp near the South African coast, a daughter was born to the Southwell family. Her father, George, was a colonel of Scottish descent serving in the British army, while her mother was French. Their infant was named Kady. As all too often happened in the nineteenth century, Kady's mother died shortly after giving birth. No one is certain whether Colonel Southwell was incapable of providing the necessary care or simply walked away from the tragic situation, but Kady was placed in the care of family friends, the McKenzies. Kady's youth was spent on the South African frontier before the McKenzies journeyed to Providence, Rhode Island, where they settled.

Like so many other young girls in New England during the 1850s, Kady found employment in a local textile mill in Central Falls, Rhode Island. It was here, as a teenager, that she met her future husband, millwright Robert Brownell, at the time a married man and the father of three children. The mutual attraction was said to be instantaneous. It was not long before Robert's wife caught wind of the affair and filed for divorce. Robert did not contest the charge of adultery, and the marriage was eventually dissolved in court. When Kady and Robert actually married remains uncertain. What is known is that Kady immediately took and retained Brownell's surname.

When the Civil War began, Robert enlisted in the First Regiment Rhode Island Volunteer Infantry. Kady wanted to accompany him no matter what the imminent danger, so she went with Robert to the steamship, boarded the vessel and then had to be forcibly removed by him prior to the vessel's departure. Undaunted, Kady paid a visit to Governor William Sprague. So impressed was he as to Kady's patriotism and determination, he allowed her passage on another steamer. After arriving in Washington, D.C., Kady found Robert and convinced him to take her along for the unknown and dangerous journey that lay ahead.

During the First Battle of Bull Run, while performing her duties as a color-bearer, Kady became separated from her husband. During the rout by the Confederates, she was led off the battlefield by a Pennsylvania soldier. Although she survived, her momentary guardian was not as fortunate. He was killed by a cannonball that tore his head off. After finding a stray horse in the woods, Kady, along with hundreds of other Union men fled back to the safety of Washington, D.C. Those without horses made the mad dash by foot. Luckily, Kady survived. Although Kady was told that Robert was killed in action, she eventually found him safe and unharmed. Both returned with their regiment to Washington and then back to Providence, mustering out after their ninety-day enlistments expired. A person would think that after the debacle at Bull Run, the Brownells would reconsider their future plans together. But their patriotism and love for each other did not fade.

Robert reenlisted in the Fifth Regiment Rhode Island Heavy Artillery. Kady followed his lead, and this time both departed with their new regiment to North Carolina under the command of Brigadier General Ambrose E. Burnside. During this campaign, Kady's reputation grew larger than life, although portions of the story may have been embellished by her and others over time.

After traveling along the Neuse River, the regiment made its way to New Bern, North Carolina. Other Union regiments that had arrived previously were surprised to see a regiment exiting the woods from a completely unexpected direction. Thinking that they were Confederates, the Union forces were nearly ready to open fire when Kady, sensing the situation, ran to the front while waving the colors. Steadfastly, she continued to advance until the Union men recognized her and her regiment as Northerners. And what was her reward? Kady was ordered to relinquish the flag to another color-bearer. Why? No one knows.

Now relegated to a more subordinate role as a nurse, Kady performed her duties with only slight protest. Make no mistake: Kady's duties still required her to administer to the fallen—Union men as well as Confederates—along breastworks that had been under heavy fire. Sometime during the battle, she learned that Robert had been severely wounded and brought to a house near the battlefield. Quickly she made her way to his side. There she administered not only to Robert but also to all the wounded soldiers at the temporary field hospital. Robert eventually spent more than eight months in the Union hospital system before receiving a discharge for his injuries. Both he and Kady returned to Rhode Island.

Not long after their homecoming, Kady and Robert moved to Connecticut. While there, Kady found a way to capitalize on her newfound fame as a war heroine by becoming an actress and performing in several theatrical productions, the most noteworthy of which, *Our Female Volunteer*, played on her war record.

While in Bridgeport, Connecticut, Kady joined the Elias Howe Jr. Post No. 3 of the Grand Army of the Republic (GAR), one of a handful of women to have been granted such an honor for her service during the war. Although there were those who questioned her wartime record and staunchly resisted her membership in the GAR, there was little they could do as Kady had received a Certificate of Discharge from the Union army. In

Kady Southwell Brownell in a post–Civil War photograph. Kady poised for a number of images wearing this homemade uniform. *Library of Congress.*

the ensuing years, she applied for and was granted a government pension of eight dollars per month by a Special Act of Congress.

The Brownells eventually moved to New York City. Here Kady worked for the park service in Central Park and later as a custodian for the Morris-Jumel Mansion.

It was during her years in New York City that her war record came under intense scrutiny. It seems that the *Providence Journal* newspaper had much to do with publicizing her bravado. But several out-of-state newspaper correspondents who interviewed veterans from her regiment refuted the magnitude of Kady's heroism, although all agreed that she certainly was present at the battles, was extremely comforting to those in need and always was resourceful and patriotic. The *Providence Journal* downplayed the accounts of the doubters. Kady's legend, though a bit tarnished, remained. Arguably, there probably are few wartime accounts of heroism that have not been embellished to some degree over time.

On January 14, 1915, at the age of seventy-two, Kady died at the Women's Relief Hospital in Oxford, New York. She was destitute. How she arrived at that state is shrouded in mystery. Robert, her husband, was aged and ill and had little money to arrange for a proper burial. Using his limited resources and with help of family and friends, Kady's remains were sent to Providence's North Burial Grounds for interment. There she lies next to Robert Brownell's first wife, Agnes. That's right: the woman who sued Robert for divorce. Why Robert chose to bury Agnes, his ex, and Kady, the adulteress, adjacent to each other was probably nothing more than simple economics. Robert died less than a year later.

Rhode Island–Born Confederates

In his fascinating work *The Civil War Book of Lists*, Donald Cartmell compiled a ranking of thirty-three Confederate officers who were born in the North. Two are Rhode Islanders: Major General Lunsford Lindsay Lomax and Colonel Lloyd J. Beall. Both men were born on separate army fortifications near Newport, Rhode Island, neither of which exists today.

Lunsford Lindsay Lomax was born at Fort Adams near the southern tip of Aquidneck Island on November 4, 1835. His father, Mann Page Lomax, was a Virginia-born ordnance officer stationed at the fort when his wife, Elizabeth Virginia, gave birth to Lunsford. The son would follow in his father's footsteps. Appointed to the U.S. Military Academy at West Point, New York, as an "at-large" candidate, Lomax graduated with a Bachelor of Science degree (a friend and classmate was Fitzhugh Lee, nephew of Robert E. Lee). His first assignment was with the U.S. Second Cavalry, serving on the western frontier. At the outbreak of the Civil War, Lomax resigned his commission to serve in the Confederacy—not a surprising move considering his family's Virginian heritage. As a captain in the Confederate army, he was assigned to the Virginia state militia under the staff of Joseph E. Johnston. Soon, he rose to the rank of lieutenant colonel.

Lomax continued his meteoric rise. After serving as a colonel in the Eleventh Virginia Calvary, he was promoted to brigadier general. Then, under his West Point classmate Fitzhugh Lee, Lomax fought at the Battle of the Wilderness and around Petersburg before his final promotion to major general. Perhaps his greatest claim to fame during the conflict was his role in the formulation of partisan bands throughout Northern Virginia that terrorized the Union army. In fact, Major John Singleton Mosby, the "Gray Ghost of Mosby's Raiders," was Lomax's subordinate.

Major General Lunsford Lindsay Lomax, Confederate States of America, in an image dated to the war. *John "J-Cat" Griffith.*

When the war ended, Lomax returned to Caroline and Fauquier Counties in Virginia, where he farmed for more than twenty years. In 1889, at the age of fifty, he was elected president of Virginia Agricultural and Mining College (now Virginia Polytechnic Institute). For reasons unknown, he was removed five years later. After working as an educator, he became a clerk at the War Department in Washington, D.C., compiling official records of both the Confederate and Union armies. He was also a member of the Gettysburg Battlefield Commission. Lomax died in Washington, D.C., on May 28, 1913, and is buried at Warrenton Cemetery in Warrenton, Virginia. He was seventy-seven.

Lloyd James Beall was born at Fort Wolcott, a fortification situated on Goat Island in the Newport Harbor on October 19, 1808, the son of Lloyd Beall and Elizabeth Waugh Jones, both of whom originally hailed from Maryland. Like Lomax, Beall was a West Point alumnus, but he graduated five years before Lomax was born. His early military career is sketchy, but by 1844, he was serving as a major in the Black Hawk

Lloyd J. Beall in a postwar engraving.
*Confederate States Marine Corps Georgia's
Company C, Savannah Sharpshooter Detachment.*

and Seminole Wars. Like Lomax, Beall's allegiance was easily swayed toward the Confederacy. Appointed first as a colonel in the Provisional Army of the Confederacy and then as colonel commandant of the Confederate States Marine Corps, Beall held the distinction of being the only individual to serve in this capacity throughout the war. In his position, he is credited with the establishment of marine training camps and permanent stations along the Mississippi River and the Atlantic coast that greatly aided the Confederate war effort.

After the conflict, Beall lived in Richmond, Virginia. Accounts note that Beall kept most of the Confederate States Marine Corps records at his home. However, a fire destroyed nearly all of the contents. Beall died on November 10, 1887, at the age of seventy-nine. Ironically, he died on the official birthday of the U.S. Marine Corps. His remains lay in Hollywood Cemetery in Richmond, Virginia, along with two U.S. presidents (James Monroe and John Tyler), Confederate States of America (CSA) president Jefferson Davis and CSA major generals George Pickett and J.E.B. Stuart.

A VALUABLE ACQUISITION?

During the war, although army regulations allowed for a cook in camp, each company mess had to find its own. On a sweltering July day, while bivouacked at Fort Alexander, Virginia, members of Company E and Company I, Tenth Rhode Island Regiment Volunteer Infantry, found theirs—or perhaps he found them. Supposedly, an African American man with an "oleaginous smile" came into camp possessing rave reviews for the job, although no one could ascertain exactly who recommended him. According to one recommendation, "He could cook anything from an egg to an elephant; either with or without fire or water." Some disagreed with the assessment. One soldier commented, "We have not had a chance to try him on the elephant, but he has certainly failed on the egg."

As to the merits of the new acquisition, one soldier explained that the cook's breakfast recipes were rather simple, complaining that boiled eggs were too soft, fried eggs were burnt on the underside and cornbread, hoecakes and johnnycakes were never browned. Sarcastically, the soldier surmised that "the chief duties of the cook were to look after number one." He added that the cook will "devour all tidbits and choice morsels, to keep them out of the way of temptation."

The new cook also foraged for food. Foraging is accomplished in a number of ways: buying provisions when you can't steal them, stealing when you can't buy them or simply stealing whether they can be bought or not. The cook usually chose the latter. He had a habit of leaving early after every breakfast, and when he returned later in the day, his plunder was usually nothing more than "a pair of meager chickens and a lank codfish." The chickens were placed in a pen for fattening, and according to one story, when time came for a good chicken soup, the broth was usually missing legs or wings. When questioned about the "deficiency," the cook had no explanation.

His biscuits turned into another misadventure. A soldier said, "We tried one, and then had the balance piled up like cannonballs."

The accounts by those in Company E and Company I left the cook's future employment open to conjecture. A wise man would argue that it was not long before he received his walking papers.

MURPHY'S LAW AND THE CAPTURE THAT LED TO THE INCARCERATION OF TWO RHODE ISLAND OFFICERS AT LIBBY PRISON

Murphy's Law struck hundreds of thousands of times during the Civil War, long before the phenomenon got its name in the twentieth century. For those needing a refresher, Murphy's Law asserts, "If anything can go wrong, it will." Allegedly, a man named Edward A. Murphy was working on an air force project to determine the amount of deceleration a person could withstand (g-force) after an abrupt stop. A test sled was designed and a pilot selected to ride in the vehicle. To monitor the results, sensors were placed at strategic locations on the test pilot's body to check such critical items as pulse, blood pressure and muscle stress. As luck would have it, the technician assigned to affix the sensors managed to attach each one in reverse order. When Murphy found out about the mistake, he was quoted as saying, "If there is any way to do it wrong, he'll find it."

Murphy was not a narcissist and did not name the incident after himself. A government project manager had already been keeping a log about the foul-ups he had witnessed in other experiments. After adding the deceleration project results to his records, he decided to call all the failures examples of "Murphy's Law." Whether this explanation is true still remains a bit of a mystery, as stories have been around for years as to the origin of the phrase. Note the following historical account.

In a study conducted more than a century ago by Alfred Holt and more recently summarized by Stephen Goranson for the American Dialectic Society, Goranson found that Holt identified a similar phenomenon without applying a grandiose name to the incidence. The year was 1877. Holt provided his findings to a gathering of men at an engineering society meeting:

> *It is found that anything that can go wrong at sea generally does go wrong sooner or later, so it is not to be wondered that owners prefer the safe to the scientific…Sufficient stress can hardly be laid on the advantages of simplicity. The human factor cannot be safely neglected in planning machinery. If attention is to be obtained, the engine must be such that the engineer will be disposed to attend to it.*

The fact remains: Murphy's Law, or whatever else anyone wants to call it, has been around since the dawn of time. For an uninformed person given a set of options, making the correct decision can prove to be like a coin toss:

Libby Prison as it appeared during the war. *Library of Congress.*

sometimes decisions are right and sometimes they are not. And when things go awry, as we have all experienced on occasion, they can prove costly and, at times, rather painful.

Consider the following examples, both of which deal with the imprisonment of two Rhode Island officers during the war: Lieutenant James M. Fales of the First Regiment Rhode Island Cavalry and Captain Thomas Simpson of Battery F, First Regiment Rhode Island Light Artillery. Each was imprisoned in Richmond's Libby Prison, one of the most notorious detention centers for Union officers in the Confederacy. But before learning about their misfortune, a brief discussion about the makeshift facility may interest the reader.

Located in Richmond's eastern end, Libby Prison, as it came to be known, was not built to hold Union prisoners. Built before the war, the prison's three brick buildings had been intended to serve as tobacco warehouses. The three buildings (East, Middle and West) were all connected by inner doors and were bounded by Cary and Dock Streets along the James River. During construction of the Middle building, the owner, John Enders Sr., founder of Richmond's tobacco industry, fell to his death from a ladder while in the structure. Whether tobacco was ever stored there still remains uncertain, but if it was, it was only for a short while.

In 1854, Captain Luther Libby leased the westernmost building from the Enders family and erected a sign advertising his business: L. Libby & Son, Ship Chandlers. After the war broke out, the buildings, like so many others in Richmond, were seized for military use. Despite Captain Libby's sudden eviction, his name would forever be associated with the infamous facility. The layout of the complex proved useful for the Confederacy. The buildings were used to hold captive Union officers and, on rare occasions, captive Union enlistees. The complex consisted of three main floors, each divided into nine separate rooms measuring about 45 feet by 105 feet in area. There was also a basement fully visible on the southern side as Cary Street sloped moderately downhill toward the James. The basement contained three large rooms. All the windows had bars. It is said that during the war, some 1,200 to 1,600 men were confined there at any given time, and by war's end, some 50,000 prisoners had experienced the harsh conditions and treatment within its confines.

Now that you know more about Libby Prison, let us examine how an unfortunate event and a wrong decision set Lieutenant Fales and Captain Simpson on the path to Confederate imprisonment. Neither happening is the slightest bit remarkable, but if you know anything about Murphy's Law, though the initial event may appear mundane, it is the second phase, the haphazard performance of a routine task or the consequence of making a wrong decision that introduces an unanticipated and undesirable result. We begin with Lieutenant James M. Fales's account.

In Middleburg, Virginia, on the night of June 17, 1863, Lieutenant Fales, while in command of Company F, First Rhode Island Calvary, along with the entire regiment managed to withstand fierce Rebel charges for more than three hours. After the final Rebel assault on the Union's right flank and rear, the entire regiment fell into disarray. While looking for his regiment in the woods in the vicinity where he expected to find it, Lieutenant Fales came upon a few Union stragglers. Asking where his regiment had gone, he was given quick directions to find it. With darkness setting in, Lieutenant Fales and his men went into camp about two miles from the initial battle scene. Because of their proximity to the enemy, Company F remained armed.

At daybreak, the order was given to mount and proceed in the direction given by the stragglers. It was then they realized that ahead lay Rebel cavalry and that another Rebel cavalry unit was positioned behind them. Realizing their advantage, the Rebels charged. Lieutenant Fales and his men had no recourse but to use their horses to jump a stone wall situated on their left flank. Then it happened. After watching his men successfully clear the hurdle, Lieutenant Fales pulled the leather reins of his horse to make the jump when the saddle slipped completely off the back of the animal. Lieutenant Fales found himself on the ground, while the horse continued to gallop. He had no other recourse than to make an attempt to run after his company. Soon, six of the Rebel cavalry were upon him. "Surrender, you damned Yankee son of a bitch!" one commanded. So began Lieutenant Fales's life as a prisoner of war.

On his march south, Lieutenant Fales met up with Captain Edward E. Chase and Lieutenant Charles G.A. Peterson from his regiment, both of whom had also became prisoners during the same engagement. After the war, commenting on their unexpected meeting, Lieutenant Fales wrote that he was "relieved to find company in my misery."

Six days after the engagement, Lieutenant Fales and the other officers found themselves incarcerated in Libby Prison with others of their own kind. Lieutenant Fales's tales of misadventure, published nearly twenty years after his capture, are filled with the usual hardships described in other journal accounts: lack of basic necessities, poor sanitation, hopeless boredom, loneliness and homesickness, coping with various illnesses and several fruitless attempts at escape. After suffering greatly, he and fellow officers were eventually exchanged. In total, Lieutenant Fales was a prisoner of the Confederate government for about one year and eight months, most of the time at Libby. As fate would have it, if it had not been for Lieutenant Fales's failure to check the tightness of his horse's saddle strap, he may never have been incarcerated at Libby Prison and forced to bear witness to its wretchedness.

Captain Thomas Simpson's story is a bit different than Lieutenant Fales's. His misfortune had nothing to do with forgetting to check his gear; rather, his mistake lay in making a wrong decision when only two options arose.

Captain Simpson was serving with Battery F, First Regiment Rhode Island Light Artillery, when his misadventure occurred. On October 27, 1864, Battery F was encamped at Jones' Landing on the James River in Virginia. On the following day, Simpson and most of the men in his battery were mustered out, as their terms of enlistment were to expire. In order to facilitate the process, Captain Simpson had to travel about three miles to Corps Headquarters to begin the necessary paperwork for separation from the service. Being in what he thought was as a secure position, Captain

Simpson and his orderly proceeded on their short journey without arms. Arriving at their destination, they found that headquarters had moved shortly before their arrival. After a few inquiries, Captain Simpson determined the general direction he should go. Five miles later, he came upon a brigade of cavalry and inquired further about directions. Because the cavalry was preparing for an engagement, he was abruptly told that it was ahead.

Here is where the story gets interesting. After traveling five hundred yards, Captain Simpson and his orderly came upon a left fork in the road. It appeared that the fork was well traveled. Captain Simpson concluded that it had to be the road the corps had taken. He was wrong. Seeing two mounted men approaching from the opposite direction, he figured that they were men from some headquarters from whom he could obtain more specific directions. Just before he was about to ask his question, he was astonished to hear: "Halt! Surrender!" With a double-barreled shotgun and a Spencer carbine pointing at him and his orderly, he made no attempt to escape. Within minutes, he was relieved of his watch. In what can best be described as hollow satisfaction, other soldiers recently captured had made the same mistake of taking the wrong road.

Captain Simpson's journey as a prisoner of the Confederates had now begun, but unlike Lieutenant Fales's, Captain Simpson's journey was short-lived and not nearly as severe. His incarceration lasted but four months before he received his parole. Had he not taken the wrong fork in the road, he most likely would have mustered out without having to experience all the Confederate hospitality extended to officers in the Union army. For Lieutenant Fales and Captain Simpson, what could go wrong did go wrong. Both men were fortunate to survive their ordeal and lived to write about their wartime experiences years later.

For those interested in learning what became of the buildings that made up Libby Prison, read on.

After Union forces occupied Richmond and released their countrymen from the prison, the buildings were used to house captured Confederates. Later, the space was occupied by a few businesses, including a fertilizer company. In 1888, a Chicago syndicate bought the complex for $23,000 with the purpose of moving it to its home state for use as a war museum. As the buildings were disassembled, each piece (wood, brick and stone) was numbered and lettered to allow for easier reassembly by construction teams in Chicago. The process was so efficient, it was said, that the reassembly went with barely a hitch. With the aid of additional capital of $400,000—along with $200,000 previously spent for dismantling, moving, reassembling and outfitting the institution with Civil War artifacts from the extensive collection of a wealthy candy manufacturer—the Great Libby Prison War Museum opened to the public.

The enterprise succeeded as a venture business for nearly a decade. Of note, the museum was in operation during the World's Columbian Exposition of 1893, although it had no connection to the extravaganza. The timing, intended or not, made the museum highly profitable during its short existence. But in 1899, the syndicate decided to close the museum possibly because it was attracting fewer visitors and losing money. The complex was disassembled again, with bricks either sold or given away as souvenirs. The Chicago Historical Society was the benefactor of the Civil War artifact collection along with bricks from the building. The bricks were used to build a Civil War Room that is still in existence today.

An Indiana farmer, Charles Danielson, from the town of Hamlet, purchased the remaining lumber and built a stock barn on his property. In 1963, the barn was torn down, and Danielson's daughter sold the lumber to Charles K. Mercer of Spencer. His intentions included reassembling the building and using it as a museum, but his plans never came to fruition. In June 1995, Mercer sold the remaining lumber to Rod Wampler of Gosport, Indiana. Each sale resulted in more and more lumber being lost to handling mishaps, rot damage due to past outside storage and, perhaps, the invasion of more souvenir hunters. Wampler eventually stored what he purchased in his barn.

Eleven years later (in October 2006), Wampler's estate placed the remaining wood up for auction. The purchaser was another Indiana fellow by the name of Robert Willey from New Haven. In a way, the man became a savior. After Willey heard that two other parties planned to bid on the lumber—a young man whose intention was to cut the artifacts into small pieces for sale on an online auction site and another who wanted the wood for floor joists—he decided to outbid the competition. Recognizing the historical value of his small find, Willey contacted authorities in Petersburg, Virginia, not far from Richmond. This led to direct talks with Pamplin Historical Park and the National Museum of the Civil War Soldier. Willey sold the lumber, mostly floor joist beams, to the park for exactly the price he paid.

Today, the remaining beams from Libby Prison are showcased at Pamplin Historical Park and the National Museum of the Civil War Soldier, the latter of which has been recently designated as a National Historic Landmark. The 422-acre park in Dinwiddie County, Virginia, along with intriguing artifacts displayed within, is well worth the visit.

Undoubtedly, the beams from Libby Prison will serve as a reminder of the hardships that Lieutenant James M. Fales, Captain Thomas Simpson and fifty thousand other soldiers had to endure—hardships that included disease, malnutrition, exposure and improper medical care.

Part IV

WAR'S END

John Wilkes Booth and Lucy Lambert Hale

Ten days before assassinating the president, John Wilkes Booth visited the fashionable resort city of Newport. Because Booth's stay was brief, the visit by the celebrated actor received little publicity. Consequently, what he was doing in Newport and his ultimate intentions are clouded in mystery, but theories abound about his visit, all unproven and impossible to corroborate.

This much is certain: Booth did visit the city on Wednesday, April 5, 1865. Why he decided to leave Washington, D.C., to visit Newport only two days after Richmond surrendered has been cause for speculation. With the exception of amateur historians, scholars have paid little attention to the visit, probably because of the lack of information about Booth's journey north.

How do we know Booth visited the city? Probably not long after the assassination, an enterprising individual had the vision to preserve the hotel ledger sheet signed by Booth when he registered at the Aquidneck House. The hotel was located on the west side of Corne Street, not far from the center of the city. Legibly signed on a large two-sided folio leaf is the following: "J.W. Booth & Lady." Booth preferred to employ a much simpler signature for this occasion, using initials of his first and middle name while not looping the

At the Aquidneck House, John Wilkes Booth registered for accommodations with his "lady" on April 5, 1865. *Newport Historical Society.*

h in his surname, which was his general practice when signing autographs for his admirers. He probably desired to remain incognito and not attract attention at a time when he was possibly finalizing plans to either kidnap or assassinate the president. Reports that surfaced after the assassination alluded to Booth's bouts of heavy drinking and a general appearance of nervousness prior to committing the crime, which may have explained his furtive behavior in Newport.

The Aquidneck House was not the oldest or largest establishment in Newport, nor was it the grandest. The Ocean House, built in 1840, and the Atlantic House, constructed in 1844, were older. Also in the surrounding area were Bateman's Boarding House, the Perry House, the Kay Street House, the United States Hotel and the Cliff Avenue Hotel. Booth had his choice of where to stay. Perhaps the Aquidneck House was chosen because it was a lovely facility where many influential visitors resided when visiting the city. Another guest that day was James Walker, a former president of Harvard College who signed the register a few entries after Booth. The hotel,

Copy of page taken from registration book at the Aquidneck House showing John Wilkes Booth's signature. *Heritage Auctions.*

located only one block east of Touro Park near the temporary quarters of the U.S. Naval Academy, was a short distance away from a multitude of ship moorings and prosperous waterfront businesses at the bottom of the hill along Thames Street and Narragansett Bay.

While Booth registered, the clerk, for whatever reason, listed his residence as Boston. He assigned the couple apartment no. 3 and wrote the letter *b*, signifying their arrival time during breakfast hours.

There has been widespread speculation as to who the "Lady" could have been. Most scholars agree that she was Lucy Lambert Hale, daughter of onetime presidential candidate and abolitionist senator John Parker Hale from New Hampshire, a vacationer to the island. Hale had been appointed by President Lincoln as ambassador to Spain.

Hale's daughter was a desirable lady. Possessing "blue eyes, dark hair, clear skin, and an attractive figure," Lucy was both sophisticated and flirtatious, with an air of aloofness that left little wonder why she received the affectionate attention of men like John Hay (Abraham Lincoln's assistant secretary), Oliver Wendell Holmes and President Lincoln's eldest son, Robert Todd, to mention a

Lucy Lambert Hale as she appeared during the Civil War. *National Park Service.*

few. But John Wilkes Booth proved to be her fancy in spite of his richly deserved reputation as a ladies' man. Lucy first met Booth in Washington a few months after he sent her an anonymous note on Valentine's Day in February 1862. Sometime after writing the note, they met. Lucy's close friends said that they were betrothed, but no announcement of the engagement was made public and much of their relationship remained secret until 1865, when they were seen more openly in public. Their love affair was not always smooth. Lucy disliked Booth's profession, and her family was said to be averse to their courtship.

Twentieth-century photographic investigators have identified John Wilkes Booth and a few of his eventual coconspirators in attendance during Lincoln's second inaugural address. Booth bragged days later that he got close enough to have killed the president if he so desired, but his escape route through such a large crowd would have been difficult. And where did Booth obtain the invitation and pass to attend the ceremony? It is believed that Lucy, with the help of her father's political connections, secured a pass not only for Booth but his associates as well. According to Lincoln scholar Edward Steers Jr., a day after the inauguration, Lucy was spending time in Booth's room at the National Hotel in Washington, D.C. Nearly one month later, Booth and his lady appeared in Newport.

Shortly after signing the hotel register at the Aquidneck House, the couple took a long walk. No one knows their topic of conversation. Upon their return, Booth asked that dinner be brought to their apartment, as his lady friend was not feeling well. When the waiter arrived with their meal, Booth and Lucy had already departed. Later that day, Booth returned to Washington. Whether he met anyone else in Newport on April 5, 1865, has been subject of wild speculation that continues to remain hearsay at best. The most frequent rumor was that Booth met with Confederate agents from Canada. However, no evidence has been found to prove the theory. Certainly, such accusations have fueled speculation and made for interesting reading.

A few accounts note that on the morning of the assassination, Booth and Lucy met in Washington, D.C. Exactly where they met remains unclear. Perhaps their final meeting is nothing more than utter speculation.

After Lincoln's assassination, Lucy was said to have remained in mourning—not for President Lincoln, but for John Wilkes Booth. Some reports place Lucy in heavy veil on the steamer *Montauk* docked in Washington when her father and other government witnesses were called to identify Booth's remains. Not long after Booth's death, Lucy's father took her to Spain, where she remained for five years, most likely to avoid scandal, before returning to the States.

After Booth was shot at Garrett's Farm in April 26, 1865, the contents of his wallet were examined. It was said to contain pictures of five ladies, one of whom was Lucy. One wonders just how captivated Booth was with her if he carried several images of attractive ladies in his possession. Booth's reputation as a womanizer remained with him until his death. After being claimed by Booth's family, his body was buried at Green Mount Cemetery in Baltimore.

John Parker Hale, Lucy's father, died in 1873. A monument in Concord, New Hampshire, has a plaque affixed that concludes with the sentence, "He who lies beneath surrendered office, place and power rather than bow down and worship slavery."

After the emotional scars healed, Lucy married William Eaton Chandler, a prominent corporate lawyer, U.S. senator from New Hampshire and later secretary of the navy. Their marriage was the first for Lucy and the second for William after his first wife had died giving birth to twins, neither of whom survived. When Lucy was forty-four years old, the couple had a child: John Parker Hall. Evidence indicates that their relationship was rocky. No one knows for certain whether Lucy ever knew anything about Booth's intentions to harm the president, although she must have been aware of his hate and discontent for the man. Before her death in 1915, Lucy requested that the letters she kept from Booth be burned. The request was honored. Lucy now rests apart from her husband at Pine Hill Cemetery, Dover, New Hampshire.

After leaving public service and the death of his second wife, Lucy, William Chandler took up residence with his eldest son by his first marriage. He died two years after Lucy's passing. Chandler is buried at Blossom Hill Cemetery in Concord, New Hampshire.

The Aquidneck House where Booth and Lucy spent a brief interlude was razed years ago. At one time, the site served as a parking lot for the Knights of Columbus, but presently, early American and colonial-style townhouses constructed to resemble eighteenth- and nineteenth-century structures occupy the spot.

Divergent Reactions to the Great Calamity

During his presidency, Abraham Lincoln was both loved and despised. It wasn't necessarily along party lines or geographical boundaries, although there were certainly more people in the South who held him in disdain. In 1865, the opposing views played out throughout the entire United States. Rhode Island was no exception.

In Providence, Frank Hail Brown (better known as Frankie), a young boy of less than five years and the son of John Adams and Ellen (Hail), took great pleasure watching soldiers drill and parade three blocks from his home on 15 Cushing Street. Frankie simply could not get enough of the pomp and ceremony, watching the soldiers marching and executing the manual of arms on the parade ground. He enjoyed it so much that his parents had a military uniform custom-tailored to fit his toddler physique. He wore it with great pride and admiration until he outgrew it.

One day in April 1865, something happened to Frankie that proved unsettling, as it would to any boy at such a young age. Although he did not thoroughly comprehend the ramification of what he heard and observed, the indelible image of what he innocently experienced that day never left him.

While being entertained, as he always was, watching soldiers performing routine drills, he noticed that one of them was sitting on the ground with hands covering his face. Gingerly approaching, he could see that the man

Armed and ready: Frank "Frankie" Hail Brown in uniform. *Henry A.L. Brown.*

was crying. Unable to fully grasp the meaning of the soldier's distressing behavior, Frankie approached him with measured steps. "Why are you crying? Soldiers don't cry," he said. The soldier looked up, tears still flowing down his cheeks, and said, "Someone has shot and killed our President." Whether there was more to the exchange between the two is uncertain. What is known is that the boy ran home shortly thereafter to tell his mother about what he saw and heard. The reaction of Frankie's mother was to be expected. "Oh no, you must be mistaken," she said, perhaps not wanting to believe what she heard or brushing it off as something her son simply misunderstood. Her reservations about the accuracy of the announcement were quickly dispelled, however, when the city's church bells begin to ring at an odd hour. Frankie had brought home the accurate but unwelcomed news of President Abraham Lincoln's assassination.

Further south in the small community of Portsmouth Grove, where an army military hospital had been established in 1862, news of Abraham Lincoln's assassination hit home like heavy artillery. When told of the reprehensible act, Dr. Lewis Edwards, the commander of Lovell General Hospital, was said to have turned pale. He blurted out what most everyone was feeling: "I can't believe it." Yet, there were those who felt the opposite.

A vendor bringing supplies from nearby Newport to the hospital made the mistake of being too verbal about his allegiance and the assassination. "Served him right," he said. "Abraham Lincoln ought to have been killed long ago." Almost immediately, the man was brought to Dr. Edwards's office to explain the disparaging remarks. Not surprisingly, his quick removal from the premises may have saved him from a lynching or beating by an angry mob of soldiers. Following a brief interrogation, one in which the vendor vehemently professed his innocence, Dr. Edwards ordered his release. But many still believed his guilt, and eventually the man lost a good trade, even if it was only to last a few more months before the hospital's official closure.

A crying soldier, a distraught commander, an outspoken purveyor…in many ways, the country was still divided after five years of war that tore through the heart of the nation. The evil and strife of war and the enduring effects of the assassination continued to resonate for years to come. Even today, there still exits a love-hate relationship whenever Abraham Lincoln's name is mentioned.

EYEWITNESS TO A TRAGIC EVENT

A packed house of 1,700 patrons was expected to attend a theatrical production that served as a benefit performance for celebrated actress Laura Keene. On April 14, 1865, John T. Ford, the theater's owner, paid for newspaper advertisements attesting that President Abraham Lincoln and General Ulysses S. Grant would be in attendance that night to view the comedy *Our American Cousin*. The advertisement was not a shill to guarantee Ford a full house, although filling the theater was certainly a prime consideration. Ford was given assurance that both men, along with their wives, would attend. But at the last minute, General Grant declined the invitation, preferring to travel with his wife to visit their daughters in New Jersey. Even without General Grant, the play would be a festive occasion—a salute to President Lincoln and the soldiers who fought bravely in the battlefields and a celebration that the terrible war had finally ended. The play went on with President Lincoln in attendance, but by the end of the night, the mood had abruptly shifted. With a single gunshot, exuberance turned into pandemonium and then grief.

One of the more fascinating books written about the half hour before, during and after Lincoln's assassination was published in 1995, titled *We Saw Lincoln Shot: One Hundred Eyewitness Accounts*. The author, Timothy S. Good, presents the verbatim accounts in chronological order from the earliest eyewitness accounts provided in April and May 1865 until the last accounts were published between 1901 and 1954. Memories can be notoriously unreliable given the length of time since the actual event. By presenting the accounts in this fashion, more credence can be attributed to the initial accounts recorded immediately after the tragedy. Although the following account is not recorded in Good's book, it is not to say the person did not witness the tragedy. There were more than two thousand patrons in attendance that evening, and not everyone gave a deposition about what they saw and heard, especially not a seven-year-old girl.

In 1910, a woman, about fifty-two years old, told a reporter with the *Providence Journal* that as a child, she was present with her parents (Mr. and Mrs. C.P. Currier) at Ford's Theatre the night President Lincoln was assassinated. Mrs. Florence A. McQuilton, a resident of 302 South Main Street in Providence, remembered the incident well. She was sitting with her family in a box directly across from the president when the shot was fired. The box was privileged seating. Because her mother was a former member and actress of the Ford Theatre Company, when the family went to Washington, D.C., they were given choice seating by the theater management.

Florence's mother was not the only actress in the family. Florence herself was an actress, having played children's roles as a youngster. On numerous occasions, she spent time in her mother's dressing room. This is how she remembered the infamous evening:

> *But I remember it as if it were yesterday. I didn't understand all that it meant, but I knew the President had been shot. Hadn't I been looking at him across the theatre, with eyes as big as saucers, because he was a real President?*

She continued:

> *The play didn't mean much to me. I shouldn't remember what it was if I hadn't read about it later. And I didn't care to look at the stage. There was nothing new about the stage for me.*

Before giving her version of the assassination, she filled in some history about the assassin:

> *Booth, the murderer, had once been my mother's basket boy, as they called them in those days. She and father knew him well. Father was one of the first to recognize him as he jumped to the stage after the shooting.*

Mrs. McQuilton then related the events of the evening in detail:

When we went into the box mother told me to look across at the opposite box. "That's our President over there," she said.

I didn't know exactly what a President was. "Is he like a king?" I asked my father. I knew about kings, because I had seen them played on the stage. Father laughed a little. He had been in the army, and I guess he loved Lincoln pretty well. "Yes, dear," he said to me, "he is a sort of king."

That was enough for me. A real king! I just sat and stared at him. I can see him now, as he sat there, with his hands crossed and sitting pretty well back in his chair, laughing and shaking his head at the play when the funny parts came, and sometimes clapping his hands. He seemed to enjoy it a lot, but he was awfully homely—oh, an awfully homely man!

Then I don't remember how long it was, I heard the pistol fired. I don't remember whether I saw the flash or not, everything happened so fast. But almost in a second I saw a man jump over the railing to the stage. There was some drapery in front of the box, and I saw him stumble in it.

He shouted as he jumped. I don't remember the words; something like "Viva le tyrant." Anyway, it was a foreign language, and I now know that it means "Death to tyrants!" but I didn't know then. I wondered what he said if for.

He shouted it just as he jumped, almost while he was in the air. No, what they say isn't right. Turn and shout it to the audience from the stage? I should say not. They'd have shot him if he had. I saw a lot of men in the audience draw pistols, but he was too quick for them.

He fell, or almost fell, to the stage, and jumped up and ran into the wings, as if he had been shot out of a cannon.

I heard father sort of catch his breath and whisper to mother, "That's Booth." You see, they both knew him well. I told you he'd been mother's basket boy, didn't I?

And then the excitement in the theatre! The yelling and shouting! The boys in the gallery screamed, "Stop him! Catch him! Catch the _____ _____!" They seemed to know what had happened before lots of people down stairs did.

But I kept my eyes on Lincoln's box. I saw him fall from his chair, or he would have fallen if the man next to him hadn't caught him. He just sank down, and Mrs. Lincoln, who had been sitting beside him, bent over him. Then the people hid the rest of what happened.

Father and mother stood up and started to go out. The stage curtain had gone down and people all over the theatre began to run down the aisles. It looked like trouble.

Then the manager came out and asked them to go out quietly and slowly, that the house wasn't on fire and that there was no danger. After that things got a little quieter. I grasped my mother's hand because I was afraid and we went out.

The next day father was away from home, hunting Booth. He was one of those who knew him well and helped identify the body after Booth was shot and before the soldiers buried him.

What do you think? Was she really there with her parents that evening? Her words certainly sound truthful and convincing.

WHEN AT FIRST YOU DON'T SUCCEED...

Criticized, sometimes mercilessly, by his military subordinates, high-ranking politicians and contemporary writers and historians, Major General Ambrose E. Burnside was called inept, stubborn, reckless, insecure, lackluster and wholly unqualified to lead the Army of the Potomac into battle. And those were only a few descriptors of what appeared to be a long list of command and personality flaws. Yet there were others who felt differently. They called him brave, loyal, honest and patriotic, with character above reproach.

Over the past several decades, Burnside's tarnished image has changed for the better. A present-day author called him "unlucky," while another said he was "a scapegoat," both of which likely hold some validity. Rising to his belated defense, some historians suggested that the general had a tendency to overly trust his subordinates—more of a "manage-by-exception" type of general. This "hands-off" style, some would argue, contributed to his demise. Others theorize that he was simply let down by his field generals or that his orders were misinterpreted. At the Battle of the Crater, Burnside's generals, Edward Fererro and James H. Ledlie, shared a bottle of rum in a bombproof shelter while their men were decimated by the Confederates. Unfortunately, Burnside paid a high price no matter who was at fault. When in command, there is no delegation of responsibility. Burnside knew this, and because of it, his military career lay in ruins.

Although failing on the battlefield—at times catastrophically and at a horrific cost in men and matériel—Burnside's tenacity enabled him to excel in Rhode Island's political arena. Returning to Bristol, Rhode Island, before the

Ambrose E. Burnside as he appeared later in life. *Author's collection.*

war concluded, Burnside became a gentleman farmer. But his new profession would not last long. The citizens of Rhode Island called on him to tackle challenges of a far different nature. Initially a Democrat, Burnside joined the Republican Party. Still greatly admired in his adopted state, Burnside was elected to three successful one-year terms as governor of Rhode Island.

The year 1871 brought many challenges for Burnside. He became the third commander-in-chief of the Grand Army of the Republic, a Civil War veterans' organization that continued in existence into the mid-twentieth century until the last veteran died. He was also the cofounder and first president of the National Rifle Association (NRA), the "Right to Bear Arms" organization that continues in the national spotlight today. Perhaps his greatest achievements in 1871 were the successful negotiations to release Americans trapped in Paris during the Franco-Prussian War and then again as an envoy to help formulate and finalize a peace agreement.

On March 5, 1875, and again on June 8, 1880, he was elected to the U.S. Senate. While in his seat, he played a key role during Reconstruction, winning the admiration of former battlefield adversaries like James Longstreet and

Wade Hampton. By this time, however, Burnside's health had begun to fail. On September 13, 1881, he died on his farm in Bristol of an apparent heart attack. He was fifty-seven years old. Burnside's remains lay in state at the Rhode Island Statehouse, Providence City Hall and the nation's capital and were viewed by thousands of mourners.

Ambrose E. Burnside, son of a former slaveholder from South Carolina, a West Point graduate and a veteran of the Mexican-American and Civil War, had fought his last battle. His remains rest at Swan Point Cemetery, Providence, Rhode Island.

RENOWNED SHAKESPEARIAN ACTOR'S SUMMER VACATION HOME

Imagine, for a moment, the absolute shock, sheer embarrassment and heavy emotional burden that was placed on the Booth family after hearing that brother and son John Wilkes had assassinated the president of the United States. That is precisely how the family felt when they received word of his infamous deed.

Edwin Booth, also a noted Shakespearian actor like his father and brothers, was performing on stage in Boston when U.S. marshals found him at the time of the assassination. He was placed under house arrest, as were other family members scattered about the country. He was questioned at considerable length, and his clothing trunk was searched for possible incriminating evidence. Nothing was found, and consequently, no charges were filed by the authorities. With his mother suffering remorse over the incident, Edwin traveled to New York to console her. Not long after, he wrote to a friend about the family's "wounded name." For months, Edwin remained indoors during daylight hours to avoid not only embarrassment but also the possibility of physical harm.

On January 3, 1866, after Edwin's absence from the stage since the previous April, his friends convinced him that the vast majority of the public held no ill feelings toward him for an act perpetrated by his deranged brother. Convinced that this was the time to reappear, Edwin returned to the stage as Hamlet in a performance held at the Winter Gardens Playhouse in New York City. His reemergence met with tumultuous applause. Those in attendance said that Edwin, while standing in the background, paused for several seconds before committing himself to his role. The audience was thrilled to have him

Edwin Booth posing as Hamlet. Booth, a famous Shakespearian actor, founded the Player's Club in New York City, which still exists today. *Library of Congress.*

back, and Edwin was once again where he belonged. Although the stigma on the family name lingered, from that day forward, Edwin's acting abilities overshadowed the emotional burden. Over the better part of two decades, Edwin performed throughout the United States and Europe to packed houses, but he never appeared again in the nation's capital.

Edwin's first marriage to Mary Devlin ended when she died of consumption at the age of twenty-three in 1863. A little more than a year earlier, Mary had given birth to a daughter, Edwina, named in honor of him. Six years later, Edwin

Left: Edwin's first wife, Mary Devlin Booth. *From* Edwin Booth.

Below: The Edwin Booth family, early 1880s. *Folger Shakespeare Library*.

remarried. His new wife was Mary McVicker. Not long after the marriage, Mary became pregnant, but their son died shortly after birth. She became withdrawn and suffered immense anguish from the loss. While her husband and his daughter traveled in Europe, Mary remained stateside. She died of the lung disease while her family was still away.

Earlier, in 1879, through the urging of his friend William Bispham, Edwin purchased three acres of land along the Sakonnet River in an area called Paradise on scenic Indian Avenue in Middletown, Rhode Island. It was a pastoral setting that overlooked Third Beach and the Atlantic Ocean. Edwin had no immediate plans for the property and kept the land undeveloped. But in 1882, while performing in Europe, Edwin decided to buy two adjacent three-acre lots with the intention of building a summer residence in the Queen Anne style of the time. According to a period account, the house was originally intended for his daughter, Edwina, who had recently become engaged to an artist. The gentleman, Downing Vaux, supposedly went insane, and the marriage never took place. After that, though construction of a cottage had commenced, it moved slowly.

In June 1883, Edwin and his daughter came to Newport to inspect the progress on building the summer retreat. During their first week back on Aquidneck Island, they stayed at the Aquidneck House in downtown Newport, the same hotel where Edwin's brother John Wilkes stayed with his "lady" in April 1865. Still under construction and with revised plans by Edwin to add two wings and a conservatory, the house was not ready for occupancy that summer. But by the following summer, the work had been completed, and Edwin and Edwina were able to move in. Edwin gave it the name Boothden. The cottage and grounds were exquisite, fit for a man of Edwin's stature.

In 1884, Edwin and Edwina became involved with fundraising activities for the Berkeley Memorial Chapel (now St. Columba's Episcopal Church), to be constructed only a short distance across the street from Booth's estate. When the cornerstone was laid, it is said that Edwina draped flowers she had picked at nearby Boothden. In honor of her mother, a stained-glass window was designed to portray a saint-like appearance of her birth mother, Mary Devlin, to be placed near the front entrance. Although Edwina was listed as the benefactor, Edwin probably footed at least a portion of the cost.

The chapel was completed and formally dedicated on Sunday, September 20, 1885. On the lower portion of the stained-glass window stand the words:

Stained-glass window donated by Edwina Booth in memory of Mary Devlin, Edwin Booth's first wife. *St. Columba's Chapel, Middletown, Rhode Island*

To the Glory of God:
and in loving memory of Mary Devlin
who fell asleep
February 21, 1863
This window is given
by her daughter Edwina Booth
AD 1885

Four months earlier, Edwina had married a Hungarian immigrant, Ignatius R. Grossman, a stockbroker by profession who never endeared himself to Edwin because of his penchant for exorbitant spending.

Although Edwin thoroughly enjoyed vacationing at the cottage, he only summered in Middletown from 1884 through 1887. Surprisingly, Edwin, Edwina and her new husband used the cottage sparingly after that. The financial constraints placed on Edwin, especially from his daughter and son-in-law's flamboyant lifestyle, made it necessary to place the property up for sale despite Edwin's belief that the real estate would eventually become a worthwhile investment. There were no takers.

While making another attempt to sell the property in 1893, Edwin suffered a stroke from which he never fully recovered. Only a few months later, he died while in the arms of his daughter at the Player's Club in New York City. The Middletown, Rhode Island cottage was subsequently bequeathed to Edwina, but along with it came substantial debt. In 1903, the bank foreclosed. Over the ensuing years, the property changed hands on numerous occasions.

According to James L. Yarnall, Boothden was used in 1929 in a sophisticated sting operation by "self-described bookies...outfitting it with fake telephones and other apparatus to impart the illusion of a big-game gambling operation." Working under the charade of rigging horse races in Florida, bookies lured wealthy out-of-town investors with promises of big payouts. When bettors came to claim their winnings, all they found was an unoccupied dwelling. The scam happened thirty-six years after Edwin's death, but if he had been alive, he may have enjoyed a chuckle over the brilliant performance. Allegedly, the successful scam served as inspiration for the 1973 movie *The Sting*, which featured Paul Newman and Robert Redford.

Today, the original cottage no longer stands. Over the past two years, Boothden has been demolished and is being reconstructed on the exact footprint of its predecessor. In many respects, the somewhat finished cottage greatly resembles Boothden during its heyday. Of the original nine-acres, only four and a half acres remain, as sales of subdivided lots have reduced its expanse but not the beauty of the location.

THE CLAIMS OF WILLIAM "BILLY" H. PARKER

In 1877, a fellow named William "Billy" H. Parker, formerly contraband of the war, moved north from Washington, D.C., and settled in rural Portsmouth, Rhode Island. What brought him and his traveling companion

Morgan Ayler to this northern island of three communities may forever remain a mystery.

Only scant clues remain about Billy's life. What is known was provided in a brief account taken from John T. Pierce Sr.'s illuminating book, *Historical Tracts of the Town of Portsmouth, Rhode Island*.

Billy Parker was born into slavery on September 1, 1848. His roots in the dreadful institution were solidified over several generations. As he grew from a boy to a young adult while laboring in the southern fields of misery, like thousands of others he realized his only hope for freedom was self-emancipation: escaping human bondage and traveling clandestinely to the North via the Underground Railroad. Other than the clothes on his back, Billy brought with him several interesting anecdotes about his family and his personal encounters as a slave.

During the Civil War, Billy claimed that his grandmother worked in the home of General Robert E. Lee, while his grandfather worked for a brother of the general. Billy's life of toil and misery culminated with his escape from bondage. As a runaway slave, he was picked up by the Union army and, like thousands of other contrabands, earned his keep doing whatever was asked of him. His first job with the army was a water boy. After making his way to Washington, he left the army and worked as an unskilled laborer to earn a living. It was in our nation's capital that Billy's story becomes interesting.

One of the first jobs Billy performed in downtown Washington was shining boots and shoes. In this role, he claimed to have shined the boots of John Wilkes Booth, not once but several times. Billy also claimed to have worked in a restaurant near Ford's Theatre and was present the night Abraham Lincoln's body was carried from the theater after the assassination. Whether he was present or not remains unsubstantiated, but if the following can be used for comparison, the likelihood of his presence at this great tragedy is lessened. For example, during the postwar period, a great number of men came forward to claim that they carried the president's body from the theater to the Peterson House directly across the street from the establishment. So many individuals claimed to have performed this task that it would have been impossible for all of them to have participated in the somber event. In fairness, Billy still may have been present to witness the happening, as many gawkers did gather outside the theater after the news of the assassination spread like wildfire throughout the streets of the city.

In his early thirties when he first settled in Portsmouth, Billy continued to find employment doing menial jobs around the town to earn a living. Finally, Billy found employment as a caretaker at Oscar Manchester's general store, located directly east and only a stone's throw from where the town library is now located. A small shed stood behind the general store. Billy was offered the space as his living quarters, and he gladly accepted. There, in his free time, he planted parsnips in a small garden on the grounds. Today, the building where the general store was located is still standing; its primary function, however, has changed over the years, as it now serves as a real estate agency. The shed that Billy called home no longer stands.

Billy lived until 1936 before passing away in his late eighties. According to Pierce's book, with nothing in Billy's estate, his last will and testament was never probated. Where he lived in the final years is unknown. He may have resided in the shed until his last breath or died as a pauper at another location.

Of interest are author John Pierce's concluding remarks about Billy. He wrote that Billy "was known for his honesty and friendliness." Perhaps Billy really did experience the events he talked about enthusiastically to residents of the community.

Although poor, Billy died a free man long after the horrors of slavery and war were behind him. But were they? Regrettably, racism was still much a part of 1930s America even in a small New England community like Portsmouth. Only after his death did William "Billy" H. Parker find lasting peace in a community that, more than likely, embraced him as one of their own—yet only at arm's length for some.

Part V

THE LEGACY

A SMALL TOWN'S SACRIFICE

In terms of sheer numbers, Providence, Cranston and Warwick, Rhode Island, suffered the greatest amount of casualties during the conflict as they were the largest cities that sent men to fight. But many of the smaller towns in the state suffered proportionate losses. Take the town of Warren, for example. Warren was a typical-size coastal community during the war, but the contribution it made and the price it paid in human terms proved as significant as those from the larger cities. Following are some specifics to illustrate the point.

Volunteers from Warren fought in many of the fiercest battles and campaigns of the war: Bull Run, the Peninsula Campaign, Antietam, Fredericksburg, Gettysburg, the Wilderness and Petersburg.

Men from Warren entered the service from many walks of life: a surgeon, an artificer (inventor), wagon drivers, musicians and a number of painters and farmers.

The Drown, Luther and Peck families were well represented, with fourteen of their sons serving in the Union army. All but one returned home from the battlefields.

Of the more than 170 men who served from the community, two were killed in action and eight succumbed to disease or illness.

Entrance to the South Burial Ground in Warren, where war veterans rest in peace. *Photo by the author.*

Fourteen soldiers were wounded in action, three of whom required battlefield amputations. One of those did not survive the trauma and subsequent infection.

James, John and Seabury Mason were three of the fourteen wounded. All recovered and returned home safely.

George E. Gardner, a black soldier from the Fourteenth Regiment Rhode Island Heavy Artillery (Colored) survived a bout with smallpox. He had the heartrending experience of witnessing the death of his brother, Joseph, from consumption in a Louisiana swamp.

Twenty soldiers were discharged for service connected disabilities either because of injury or illness.

One soldier had the dubious distinction of being dishonorably discharged.

Nine soldiers were prisoners of war. Benjamin F. Hiscox was taken prisoner twice and eventually died of an undisclosed illness in a Confederate prison. His brother, Sylvester, was also taken prisoner but managed to survive the ordeal and was exchanged. Sylvester continued to fight for the Union until the war's end, perhaps to honor his brother's memory.

MEMORIAL DAY

Memorial Day was not always called Memorial Day. On May 5, 1868, the commander of the Grand Army of the Republic, Major General John A. Logan, established May 30 as Decoration Day to pay tribute to fallen Union soldiers by placing flowers on their graves. The date selection was not arbitrary. The end of May coincided with flowers being in bloom throughout the country. Supposedly, the first veteran graves to be decorated in the North were at Arlington National Cemetery. Both flowers and small flags were used to honor the dead. The first ceremony at Arlington was attended by five thousand people. Today at Arlington, the number paying tribute to deceased veterans on Memorial Day is about the same.

But wait. Women from Columbus, Mississippi, claimed to have decorated the graves of Southern soldiers who lost their lives at Shiloh as early as April 25, 1866. Although their intention was to honor the Confederate dead, the ladies were saddened that Union graves were neglected, so they also placed flowers on these graves. It was a fitting and noble gesture.

Does the story end here? No, it does not. Macon and Columbus, Georgia, along with Richmond, Virginia, claim to have proof that veteran graves were decorated earlier than they were in Mississippi—as much as two years earlier, while the war was still raging. Boalsburg, Pennsylvania, also lays claim to being the first. And if one travels to a particular cemetery in Carbondale, Illinois, one would see a stone that claims that the first Decoration Day ceremony was held there. In fact, more than twenty-five cities and towns (mostly in the South) lay claim to being the first to establish the day of remembrance.

In 1966, Congress and President Lyndon Johnson declared Waterloo, New York, as the official birthplace of Memorial Day. The date of May 5, 1866, was a few weeks later than what the women in Mississippi could attest, but in Waterloo, the day was a much larger event than the simple placing of flowers or small flags on graves. In Waterloo, businesses closed and flags were flown at half-staff. What swayed Congress was that Waterloo had continually observed the day of remembrance right up to the present and that it was always conducted as a community-wide affair (the year 2013 will mark the 147th consecutive observance of Memorial Day by the residents). Of course, when you win the war, you can also establish the selection criteria.

Which side could lay claim to being first is actually a moot point. The fact that citizens from both the North and South recognized the importance of honoring their fallen war heroes is the primary consideration and one of several factors that began the reconciliation process; as the joys of life bring people together, so does the sadness of death.

New York was the first state to recognize Memorial Day as a holiday, followed by Rhode Island in 1874. In the meantime, states throughout the nation issued proclamations designating May 30 as Memorial Day. The army and navy also set guidelines for the day's observance at their installations. But not until World War I was the day celebrated to honor all deceased veterans who served in any American war.

The North and the South were certainly not the first to honor their war dead. The honoring of fallen heroes goes back at least twenty-four centuries, to the time of the Peloponnesian War, if not before.

In Rhode Island, during the late nineteenth and up to mid-twentieth century, all twenty-four of the state's Grand Army of the Republic posts observed the holiday in earnest. On the Sunday before Memorial Day, members of the GAR dressed in their finest uniforms and attended church services, where they heard patriotic sermons. On Memorial Day, the members also attended outdoor services after gathering at the Soldiers and Sailors Monument on Exchange Place in Providence. From there, GAR members marched to a dirge up Westminster Street to pass in review for the GAR department commander. Lining the streets were scores of citizens. After reaching Exchange Place, they placed flowers at General Burnside's statue before being officially dismissed. Members then departed in separate contingents to cemeteries throughout the state to decorate the graves of their fallen comrades.

In the weeks ahead, the department chaplain was charged with the responsibility of analyzing the effectiveness of the proceedings. In a report for the year 1908 documenting Memorial Day the previous year, he recorded the following: 746 members (54 percent) attended church services; 142 cemeteries were visited for grave decorations; 6,007 graves were decorated; fifty-eight public schools engaged in services, with 2,000 students participating; and sixty-two other organizations helped with the proceedings. Rhode Island continued to do its duty by remembering its fallen comrades.

But then, about eighty years later, Congress passed the National Holiday Act of 1971 (P.L. 90-363) that ensured a three-day weekend for all federal holidays. Memorial Day was now observed on the last Monday in May and no longer on the thirtieth. Although the purpose of the holiday had diminished over the years, the situation had worsened. A new generation of Americans either lost or never understood the significance of the day. For surviving veterans, it was a hard pill to swallow. Although there have been efforts to restore Memorial Day to May 30, Congress has shown little interest

On Memorial Day in 1937, aged Civil War veterans gathered in Providence, Rhode Island, to attend ceremonies as members of the Department of Rhode Island GAR. *State of Rhode Island and Providence Plantations, Office of the Secretary of State, Archives Division, Providence, Rhode Island.*

in doing so. The fact remains that average citizens look forward to extended time with their family and friends away from the stress of work. In 2002, during a Memorial Day address, a Veterans of Foreign Wars official said, "Changing the date merely to create three-day weekends has undermined the very meaning of the day. No doubt, this has contributed greatly to the general public's nonchalant observance of Memorial Day."

In January 1999, Senator Inouye introduced a bill in the U.S. Senate to restore May 30 as the traditional day of observance. Three months later, Representative Gibbons introduced the bill to the U.S. House of Representatives. The bill was then referred to the Committee on the Judiciary and the Committee on Government Reform. Here the bill has languished for more than a decade, and there is nothing new to report.

The situation may not be as bleak as it appears. A resolution was passed in December 2000 that calls for a moment of silence at 3:00 p.m. local time for all

Americans on Memorial Day to "voluntarily and informally observe in their own way a Moment of remembrance and respect, pausing from whatever they are doing for a moment of silence or listening to 'Taps.'" It is called the National Moment of Remembrance Act. As founder Carmella LaSpada said, "It's a way we can all help put the memorial back in Memorial Day."

In Providence, some fifty years after the war ended, the department commander of the GAR said, "Let us, as long as our great Commander gives us strength, perform this loving duty of Memorial Day, and when the time comes when we are no longer able to fulfill this trust, let our sons and daughters take up the work where we lay it down." He knew that the days of Civil War veterans were numbered. In 1890, there were 2,944 filling the ranks of the organization. By 1912, the number had dwindled to 1,283. The day finally came when *others* were called to carry the torch of remembrance.

Who are the others? One has only to look in a mirror. All of us, young and old, male and female, civilians and military, have a responsibility to observe the holiday as originally intended by honoring those who sacrificed their lives for the freedom that today we so richly enjoy.

RHODE ISLAND SOLDIERS HOME

In the late 1880s, the "boys" who fought in the Civil War were now getting along in years. Some suffered debilitating health issues in an age when health insurance was nonexistent. Others were homeless and destitute. Some were chronic alcoholics and heavy drug users—beer, wine, whiskey, opium and morphine were administered to the sick and wounded as stimulants and painkillers at field and general hospitals throughout the war years. Many were burdens to their families—that is, if they had families. Arguably, these veterans lived a precarious existence, and the only solution seemed to be sending them to poor farms as wards of the town or state. There they languished until death, an ending that provided the only means of escape. No veterans wished or deserved such a fate, but the cruel reality was that there was nowhere else for them to turn.

In Rhode Island, a group of concerned citizens recognized the seriousness of the issue and the urgency of helping these veterans. A committee was formed made up of Civil War veterans and current military staff and politicians from the state to look into the matter. The committee recommended the establishment of a veterans home for those unable to provide for their own well-being.

In April 1889, the state formed a board and immediately tasked it to find a suitable location on which to build the home. The board felt that its best option was to place newspaper advertisements seeking public input about where the veterans home should be built. There were twelve responses, with two offering land donations for the home. The Town of Bristol offered three different sites, all free of charge. In a meeting held on July 12, 1889, the one-hundred-acre Green Farm on Metacom Avenue in Bristol was selected as the site of the proposed home (the farm was originally owned by Davis Wilson, who bequeathed it to the town upon his death). In the summer of 1889, after the General Assembly and the Town of Bristol approved the land donation to the state, a title dispute arose, causing a delay in construction. Because the need was pressing, a temporary facility was established in the village of Wickford. That home opened in October 1889 and, from its inception, was already operating at full capacity, with thirty-six residents calling it home. Those who could not get in—and there were many—were placed on a waiting list.

After visiting other state-run veterans homes, the Rhode Island committee decided to copy a "pavilion" building concept used successfully by the State of New Jersey, with Arthur L. Almy as the architect. His design employed the Queen Anne concept, using elegant but simple touches that was fashionable in the late 1800s. Rhode Island's plan called for an administration and a domestic building connected by walkways with an overhanging roof. The administration building would include public and private offices, a surgeon's office, an examination room and dispensary, a parlor, a dining room and sleeping quarters for the executive officer. The domestic building would contain a dining hall, a kitchen, a library, an amusement and smoking area and sleeping quarters for the kitchen personnel. The pavilions were to be single story and accommodate thirty cots along with an area for a small wardrobe or locker, rooms for ward masters and supervisors and a lavatory and water closets. Another pavilion would include a laundry on one side and eight bathtubs on the other. There would be a chapel built to hold two hundred worshipers. There would also be separate buildings for privies and a morgue. With the exception of the morgue, which was to be built of brick and stone, all the other buildings were to be constructed of wood. The commandant and his family were allocated separate quarters. There was also a boiler house and a sixty-six-foot-high water tower. The tower still stands today, and the water pump remains in working order. When the facility was completed more than a year later, it cost the state $139,000.

An early postcard showing the Rhode Island Soldiers Home. *William "Bill" Camara Jr., the State of Rhode Island, Department of Human Services, Division of Veterans Affairs.*

As a disabled or disadvantaged veteran, getting into the home was not easy. To be accepted as a resident, applicants had to meet a number of requirements:

- Be a resident of Rhode Island on April 23, 1889;
- Be an honorably discharged soldier or sailor of the Civil War;
- Be unable to support himself because of wounds, disease or other infirmities;
- Have no one to support him such as immediate family, relatives, or friends;
- If a pensioner, be required to surrender the entire sum less $4.00 per month to the State Board of Soldiers' Relief;
- While residing at the home, conduct himself in a quiet and orderly manner; and
- That the veteran was subject to discharge from the home for habitual intoxication or disobeying orders by the person in charge.

When the facility opened, thirty-six soldiers became the first residents, but soon a waiting list grew and additional buildings were needed to handle the demand. An annex was added in 1893, and another pavilion was built five years later.

By 1892, there were 152 veterans living at the home. Statistically, one-third were foreign-born, and 86 percent were literate—about the national average; 38 were single, 42 were married (apparently their wives were unable to care for them), 63 were widowed and 9 were divorced. Their trades and professions varied greatly. They were barbers, carpenters, jewelers, musicians, teamsters and weavers. About 32 percent were common laborers.

For the most part, the home became a self-sustaining enterprise. The grounds contained a thirty-acre vegetable garden, a dairy herd and a piggery, all of which helped to supplement provisions that previously had been bought from outside vendors. These ventures also reduced the operating cost of the institution.

Each year, the commander of the Rhode Island Grand Army of the Republic (GAR) toured the facility. In the *Forty-First Annual Encampment Report*, the commander noted that he had visited the home twice the past year and found everything to be in order, commenting that "it seems to me…the veterans are very fortunate in having such a pleasant place and such good care to pass the remainder of their lives."

Over the ensuing years, a surgeon's cottage was built and several wings added. Although a kitchen fire on January 31, 1911, destroyed some of the buildings, they were rebuilt as expeditiously as possible.

By 1935, a number of veterans from the Spanish-American War and World War I were carried on the rolls at the home, while only a few Civil War veterans remained. Most had passed away years earlier. In 1937, only a single GAR veteran was living there. His name was Jeremiah J. Hopkins.

During World War II, the Rhode Island legislature determined that the existing buildings at the Soldiers Home no longer conformed to safety and fire codes. This required the demolition of many of the outdated buildings. Immediately, the construction of a new brick and masonry hospital and dormitory commenced. Another building was added in 1955. At that time, the hospital was renamed. It was to be called the Rhode Island Veterans Home. Over the next several decades, a number of additions were added, such as infirmary wings, a physical occupational therapy unit, a dental office, an X-ray room, a pharmacy, laboratories, a dietary unit, a kitchen and a library. In 1976, a new nursing wing was added, creating room for another 150 residents. In 1989, another wing was constructed to accommodate thirty-six additional beds. Today, the facility also offers rehabilitation, social and transitional services along with enhanced recreational facilities, a barbershop, a beautician parlor, a gift shop, a café and a bank.

On the November 6, 2012 ballot, citizens of Rhode Island overwhelmingly approved a bond issue that authorized the state to issue bonds not to exceed $94 million for the construction of a new veterans home along with much-needed renovations to the existing facilities that could be salvaged. Any federal funds received for the same purpose would be used to offset the amount of bonds originally requested. Present-day and future veterans who need the facility will continue to receive the best healthcare possible—something they richly deserve for honorable, dedicated and gallant service to their country.

THE LAST SURVIVING GRAND ARMY OF THE REPUBLIC VETERANS FROM THE STATE

The Grand Army of the Republic (GAR) was founded on April 6, 1866, by Benjamin F. Stephenson in Decatur, Illinois. This fraternal organization was composed of veterans of the Union army, navy, marines and Revenue Cutter Service. During its existence, the GAR became an influential advocacy group for its members, championing causes such as the right to vote for blacks and veteran pension benefits, to name but a few. The group also was a major influence in maintaining patriotic activities throughout the country. In 1890, during its peak, the organization claimed 490,000 members.

The Rhode Island chapters of the GAR reached a high of twenty-seven instate posts before leveling off to twenty-four, a number maintained for several decades. Each post had its own commander, who, in turn, reported to the department commander of the entire state. From 1866 on into the 1940s, its members attended national encampments, held throughout the country with the exception of the South, for obvious reasons. The Department of Rhode Island GAR also held its own statewide encampments.

During the month of May 1937, sandwiched between articles about the *Hindenburg* airship disaster at Lakehurst, New Jersey, and the coronation of King George VI of Great Britain, the *Providence Journal* published bylines by George F. Troy Jr. that paid tribute to the last surviving Department of Rhode Island GAR war veterans who lived in the state. Following are some facts about the veterans, along with a few tidbits of what they remembered and told the reporter:

CHARLES H. BULLOCK, EAST PROVIDENCE
(TWENTY-SECOND REGIMENT MASSACHUSETTS VOLUNTEER INFANTRY)
According to those who knew the surviving GAR veterans, Bullock, even at age 96, seemed to be the spryest of the entire group. Bullock joined the Union army in spite of his father's silent allegiance to the Confederacy. Not remembering much about the war, he did remember a sad generalization: "a lot of men died that might have been saved if there'd been the right kind of medical care," he said. Reflecting further, he remembered seeing "wounded men, still breathing, tumbled into the trenches and buried because it was figured they'd die anyway."

RODMAN CARPENTER
(U.S. NAVY)
Like many a boy, Carpenter ran away from home for adventure. In Carpenter's case, he joined the Union navy as a cabin boy. During his conversation with the reporter, he referred to his boat as "the bloody Lackawanna." His ship was part of an 18 vessel flotilla that ran the gauntlet of Fort Morgan and a torpedo-infested bay near Mobile, Alabama. Carpenter was left permanently deaf from the noise of cannon fire after one particular engagement.

HENRY L. ESTEN, CHEPACHET
(SIXTY-SECOND REGIMENT MASSACHUSETTS VOLUNTEER INFANTRY)
When Esten enlisted, he had 86 cents in his pocket. Though underage, he passed for someone older. When Esten's father found out that he joined the army, he was "hopping mad." When his father found him in Worcester, he spoke to the commanding officer and demanded that his son be released. The officer agreed but said, "When the boy is home I'll come down and swear out a warrant charging him with perjury in giving his age." All went silent. The father turned around and immediately departed for home; his son was not in tow. But it was not long before the son reunited with his dad. A month later, General Lee surrendered, and Esten soon returned home without firing a shot in anger.

JOHN W. HOLLIHAN, WEST WARWICK
(FIRST REGIMENT RHODE ISLAND LIGHT ARTILLERY)
Hollihan was captured by Confederates during the Battle of the Crater. Prior to the mine disaster at Petersburg, Hollihan had fought on a number of battlefields and suffered at least one serious injury that sidelined him for seven weeks. But Hollihan was more anxious to tell the reporter another non-battle story. When he left Washington, DC to come home, he not only saw but shook hands with President Lincoln. "I walked right over to him," he said. Two days later, Hollihan learned that President Lincoln had been assassinated.

One of the last GAR veterans from Rhode Island: Jeremiah J. Hopkins. From George F. Troy Jr.'s article "Rhode Island's Boys in Blue," *Providence Journal*, May 10, 1937. *Copyright © 2012, the Providence Journal. Reproduced by permission.*

JEREMIAH J. HOPKINS, BRISTOL
(FIRST REGIMENT RHODE ISLAND LIGHT ARTILLERY)
When interviewed at the state's soldiers home, Hopkins reminisced about First Bull Run: "I remember McDowell ridin' by in the thick of it. He wasn't no further off than that wall, and he says, 'Boys, don't give up this time or the country will never forgive us.' And it wasn't two minutes later when we were all putting across Bull Run with rebels after us." The Union rout had started and Hopkins had no shame when telling his story.

STEPHEN H. KETTLE, COVENTRY
(SECOND REGIMENT RHODE ISLAND VOLUNTEER INFANTRY)
The Providence Journal *reporter found Kettle in his potato patch and when approached, Kettle was "whistling a tune that sounded faintly reminiscent of the fife and drum." Kettle was 91. When the reporter asked Kettle if he would talk about some of his wartime experiences, he was more than happy to oblige. Kettle fought in a number of skirmishes like Hatcher's Run, Fort Stedman, Fort Fisher, and Sailor's Creek. Like his comrades, he was saddened by the loss of so many GAR members over the past year.*

DR. CHARLES H. LEONARD, PROVIDENCE
(FORTY-FIFTH REGIMENT MASSACHUSETTS VOLUNTEER INFANTRY)
Dr. Leonard was a student at Yale University when the war broke out. Looking for excitement, he joined the infantry. Leonard was discharged after nine months in the service after contracting typhoid fever, but not before witnessing a man getting his face blown away. "I did plenty of ducking after that," he said.

CHARLES H. LEWIS, PAWTUCKET
(FIRST REGIMENT RHODE ISLAND LIGHT ARTILLERY)
Charles's father was concerned that his son, only fourteen years old, had to carry a drum that was too heavy for him. So the soldiers in the unit pitched in and collected $40.00 for a lighter one. According to Lewis, "I carried that drum right up to Lee's surrender at Appomattox," and that "he would not take $1,000 for it if he still had it." After Appomattox, Lewis noticed that the drum "got heavier and heavier." Eventually, on his way home, he tossed it in a river.

Civil War veterans walk together as their photograph is taken for posterity. *Department of Rhode Island Sons of Union Veterans of the Civil War.*

DAVID MILLS, SHANNOCK
(REGIMENTAL AFFILIATION UNCONFIRMED)
Mills was described as a man who could "loosen rafters" when he laughed. His easygoing manner meshed well with his physical characteristics: short and stout. He also loved to smoke his corncob pipe. But his humor and external disposition hid the fact that he served in over twenty-two separate engagements in the war. On one occasion, he told about receiving an order to charge over the parapet: "I had a lot more hair then than I've got now, and I guess that's what saved me. Anyway this bullet comes—whoosh! Right across the top of my head…I fell back into the trench and all the boys they started hollering; 'Mills is killed.' But I jumps up and says 'No, I ain't.'" Again, he made a second attempt to charge. "Another bullet comes along and chunks into my knapsack. It hit that pork [a piece of salted meat he had previously tucked away] *and I went down again!" he laughed.*

JOSEPH T. RAY, NEWPORT
(THIRTY-EIGHTH REGIMENT U.S. COLORED TROOPS)
Ray, a black soldier, hailed from Bristol, Rhode Island. At the age of 18, he and some friends decided to enlist before the war ended. One month later, it did. When he was interviewed by The Providence Journal *reporter, Ray had just finished cutting the lawn. He was 90 years old and was being chastised by his daughter for doing such hard work. She said to the reporter, "He can't stand inactivity." When entering Ray's home, the reporter noticed a nicely framed document on the wall. For years it had been one of his most prized possessions: an honorable discharge certificate.*

GEORGE H. SPAULDING, CENTRAL FALLS
(FIRST REGIMENT RHODE ISLAND CAVALRY)
During the war, Spaulding had the dangerous job of a dispatch rider that brought him into contact with high-ranking generals such as Grant, Burnside, Hooker, and Sheridan. During the interview, he recalled a raid conducted on a Southern family that had just sat down for Christmas dinner. The empty stomach marauders "cleaned up the turkeys, and about everything edible in sight." After 3 years and 11 months of military life, Spaulding's regiment took part in the final campaign of the war that ended with General Lee's surrender at Appomattox.

AMASA P. TABER, WEST WARWICK
(FIRST REGIMENT RHODE ISLAND LIGHT ARTILLERY)
When interviewed, Taber was more talkative about the friends he recently buried then his service in the artillery. Taber did talk about his time in training when he and twenty-six others were stricken with spinal meningitis. Only he and two others survived. He credited his survival on a friend; Jeremiah J. Hopkins who watched over him for two months. "I'll never forget that," he said.

EDWARD B. TAYLOR, WEST WARWICK
(SECOND REGIMENT U.S. COLORED TROOPS)
Taylor was a slave on a Maryland plantation when he first heard menacing gunfire far to his south that lasted the entire day. It was a rainy Sunday and it didn't take long for the slaves to surmise that a battle was taking place not far from their shanty homes and fields. Soon afterward, Taylor fled, made his way unscathed to Washington, DC, and joined the Union army. When interviewed by the reporter, Taylor had a hard time remembering much about his war years. His wife and daughter filled in some of the blanks. But when the reporter asked about his GAR post and his old friends, he seemed to perk up. He remembered names then spoke them aloud. Falling back into his chair, he said, "Ain't many left now. They're dropping fast," all the while shaking his head.

ELISHA R. WATSON, COVENTRY
(SEVENTH REGIMENT RHODE ISLAND VOLUNTEER INFANTRY)
At the Battle of the Crater at Petersburg, Watson told of his experience that catastrophic day: "The Colonel's artificial leg was shot away and he thanked his stars it wasn't his good one. A couple of the boys supported him while he urged us on. The rebel brigade charged but we fought back. I couldn't see losing what ground we had gained." Watson told the reporter that he fired his musket at least seventy times before a round jammed halfway down the muzzle. Finally, the colonel raised a white flag and many Union men were taken prisoner. Watson spent the next seven months at Danville Prison.

The last black survivor of the Department of Rhode Island GAR: Edward B. Taylor. George F. Troy Jr., "Rhode Island's Boys in Blue," *Providence Journal*, May 24, 1937. *Copyright © 2012, the* Providence Journal. *Reproduced by permission.*

For whatever reason, three other GAR members from the state were not interviewed by the reporter: Charles E. Ballou of Pawtuxet Valley (Ninth Regiment Rhode Island Volunteer Infantry), Thomas S. Hudson of Newport (First Regiment Rhode Island Cavalry) and John H. Riley. Riley, formerly a soldier with Company H, Second Regiment Rhode Island Volunteer Infantry, was no more heroic than any other veteran from the state, but he did hold a unique distinction. Riley was considered by many to be the last surviving member of the Department of Rhode Island GAR. Born in Dover, New Jersey, in 1841, he died just shy of his 102nd birthday. The pains of war were very familiar to him. His father was killed at the Battle of Bull Run, and his brother was seriously wounded on the same battlefield. Riley enlisted in 1863 and eventually saw action at Gettysburg, Sailor's Creek, Fort Steadman and Fort Fisher, to name only the major encounters. When General Lee surrendered to General Grant at Appomattox Court House in Virginia, Riley was at the scene and remembers firing a parting salute at the close of the war. He also held vivid memories of seeing President Lincoln on numerous occasions in Washington, D.C. After returning home, Riley held several jobs—as a stagecoach driver, a carpenter and a millwright. In his lifetime, he fathered eleven children. A few months before he died on May 7, 1943, Riley was named department commander of the GAR in the state, the last to hold the honor. His remains rest in Scituate, Rhode Island.

Unlike other veterans organizations of today, such as the Veterans of Foreign Wars, the Disabled American Veterans and the Military Order of the Purple Heart, with veterans who served in different wars, membership in the GAR "was strictly limited to 'veterans of the late unpleasantness.'" As members died off, so did the organization, first slowly and then dreadfully fast. The GAR was dissolved in 1956 when its last member died: James

Woolson. (Woolson was a drummer boy with the First Regiment, Minnesota Heavy Artillery. He passed away at the age of 109 in Duluth, Minnesota. Neither he nor his unit ever saw combat.)

Interesting to note, the last black comrade to die from the Department of Rhode Island GAR was Edward B. Taylor, the former slave mentioned previously. Although suffering from dementia, Taylor actively participated in many statewide GAR functions right up to his passing.

The GAR knew that the day would come and, therefore, made preparations to hand the reins to a different generation of men, many of whom would see combat in subsequent wars. In 1878, the GAR founded the Corps of Cadets, which in 1881 became known as the Sons of Veterans of the United States of America (SV). In 1925, the organization changed its name to the Sons of Union Veterans of the Civil War (SUVCW). Still in existence, the SUVCW maintains posts throughout the North. In Rhode Island, there are several camps chartered by the national organization. One of the groups, the Elisha Hunt Rhodes Camp 11, Sons of Union Veterans of the Civil War, has been diligent in hosting numerous patriotic activities throughout the state, such as statewide school programs, placing flags at veterans graves on Memorial Day, organizing a graves registration database of Civil War veterans, rededicating important sites relating to the Civil War within Rhode Island and disseminating information about its Civil War veterans. Of special interest, the Cranston, Rhode Island headquarters of the SUVCW is in the process of outfitting a museum that will house the organization's GAR collections, such as war relics, veterans memorabilia, period veterans' letters, books, artwork, photographs and other Civil War–related items.

QUESTION WHAT YOU SEE

Many present-day historians have learned that a surprising number of images taken during the conflict were initially misidentified due to lapses in the original photographer's memory while processing a massive number of images in the field. It is hard to find fault knowing the difficulties these pioneering photographers encountered. Perhaps the battlefield images were correctly annotated by the photographer but were subsequently mishandled by others and, as years passed, lost their true identities. Honest mistakes were made. Not so honest, however, were the so-called professionals who purposely staged shots to show greater horror, thus making each image more marketable. By appealing to the morbid fascination of the general and highly gullible public, sales of such images could be increased tenfold.

The truth is that scholars and historians have been duped as much as laymen. In the June 2012 edition of *Civil War Times Magazine*, the editor pointed out that an image passed off as "one of the few known photographs of Confederates in field uniform taken after the early part of the war" exhibits problems that bring into question its authenticity.

But finding deceptions in Civil War photographs dates back decades. While carefully examining images taken in the vicinity of Devil's Den on the Gettysburg battlefield in 1961, Frederic Ray, art director of *Civil War Times Illustrated* magazine, ascertained that a Confederate body was moved by photographers from its original position before being propped against a stone wall several yards away. The resultant image they took was both ghastly and, in a macabre way, eloquent. Almost instantaneously, the photograph became a classic. The article documenting Ray's findings first appeared in the magazine as, "The Case of the Rearranged Corpse." William A. Frassanito, perhaps the most credible and well-known forensic investigator of Civil War photographs, visually highlighted Ray's findings in his book, *Gettysburg: A Journey in Time*.

As happened after most Civil War battles, photographers arrived late on the scene, sometimes days after much of the morbid cleanup had been accomplished, particularly after a Northern victory. Bodies were hard to find, as most of the Union dead had already been buried. Some say, though with reservation, that pictures of Confederate dead strewn on the battlefield might have been purposely misidentified as Union soldiers killed in action.

Over the past twenty to thirty years, through sheer perseverance and painstaking research, a number of photographs have been scrutinized not because of suspected fraud but simply because better-trained scholars with more effective tools at their disposal have begun to question images that just didn't seem quite right. In one case, a photograph captioned as the USS *Agawam* was proven to be the USS *Mackinaw*. In another, historians discovered that a crowd scene originally identified as an image taken during President Ulysses S. Grant's inauguration was actually taken at President Abraham Lincoln's second inauguration. And what is perhaps one of the most fascinating images repeatedly published in books and magazines depicts a company of Union soldiers sitting in a trench formerly occupied by Confederates. Officers can be seen standing on a dirt embankment peering out at open terrain. For years, the location was thought to be near Petersburg, but in fact, it is an image taken on April 29 or 30, 1863, a year earlier, at Deep Run.

As you might expect, Rhode Island has its own Civil War image that came under critical review in 1992. Although the caption is not entirely misleading, it is inaccurate. Civil War author and historian Mark Dunkelman explained:

> The familiar photograph reproduced here depicts the departure from Providence, Rhode Island, of one of the state's first military units to leave for the front during the Civil War, just days after the April 13, 1861, surrender of Fort Sumter.
>
> This famous photograph has been reproduced several times, most often credited to the collections of the Rhode Island Historical Society. I readily located it in five heavily-illustrated histories of the war from my personal library. The earliest appearance was in Francis T. Miller's 1911 Photographic History of the Civil War (Vol. VIII, p. 60); the latest in Geoffrey C. Ward's 1990 The Civil War: An Illustrated History (pp. 50–51), the companion volume to Ken Burns's popular PBS television series, which utilized Rhode Island sources (notably the Sullivan Ballou letter and Elisha Hunt Rhodes's diary) to such good effect. Between those two sources, I found the Providence photograph reproduced in The American Heritage Picture History of the Civil War (1960, p. 73); The Image of War 1861–1865 (1981, Vol. I, Shadows of the Storm, p. 144); and Time-Life Books' First Blood (1983, pp. 40–41). No doubt the photo has been published elsewhere. The popularity of the image is not surprising, because it's one of the best available depictions of Civil War troops leaving home for the front.
>
> The way the photograph has been captioned through the years raises some questions, however. The caption in Miller's is quite specific: "THE FIRST RHODE ISLAND INFANTRY LEAVING PROVIDENCE, APRIL 20, 1861. The sidewalks were filled with cheering throngs, and unbounded enthusiasm greeted the volunteers, as the first division of the First Regiment of Detached Rhode Island Militia left Providence for Washington on April 20, 1861. At 10:30 in the morning Colonel Ambrose Burnside, in command, had ordered the men of the first division to assemble upon Exchange Place. The band was followed by the National Cadets and the first division was led by Colonel Burnside himself. It contained practically half of each of the ten companies, six of which were recruited in Providence and one each in Pawtucket, Woonsocket, Newport, and Westerly. The second division left four

A second detachment of the First Regiment Rhode Island Infantry departs Providence, Rhode Island, on April 24, 1861. *From* Photographic History of the Civil War.

days later. The men in this photograph marched through Exchange Street to Market Square, up North Main Street and through Meeting to Benefit, and down Benefit to Fox Point." But, as William C. Davis points out in the introduction to the Image of War *series, the editors of Miller's reproduced "scores, if not hundreds" of photographs over erroneous captions—"errors that have been accepted and passed on by the hundreds of books since 1911 that have drawn upon Miller." Which begs the question: is the caption in Miller's accurate?*

The captions in the newer books are annoyingly vague, or downright inaccurate. The American Heritage book simply states, "Colonel Ambrose Burnside led the Detached Rhode Island Militia out of Providence." Davis's Image of War *series declares, "In April 1861, the 1ˢᵗ Rhode Island Infantry marched to the railroad depot in Providence to ride to the South, their governor, William Sprague, at their head." The incorrect assumption had been made that the troops were transported via railroad—an understandable assumption, because they are assembled in front of Providence's railroad station, the Romanesque brick structure at the right of the photograph. The Time-Life series repeated the railroad depot mistake, and compounded it by implying that the entire regiment is depicted: "One thousand troops of the 1ˢᵗ Rhode Island Infantry march past a cheering throng to the Providence railroad station en route to Washington,*

D.C." The Ward/Burns book uses the photo as a backdrop to an inset of Elisha Hunt Rhodes of the 2nd Rhode Island, with the comment, "On his way to Washington, he [Rhodes] marched through Providence, cheered by many of the same citizens who had turned out to see the 1st Rhode Island off to war two months earlier"—displaying the same cavalier treatment of photographs as historical documents that was oftentimes evident in their TV series.

To complicate the mystery, let's turn to Patrick Conley and Paul Campbell's 1982 Providence: A Pictorial History, which includes the photo (p. 87) with this caption: "This April 24, 1861, photo depicts the departure from Providence's Exchange Place of the second wave—510 men—of the First Rhode Island Regiment of Detached Militia, Lieutenant Colonel Joseph T. Pitman commanding. The initial wave of 530 men had left with Governor Sprague four days earlier." And so Conley and Campbell completely contradict the caption Miller assigned to the photograph.

The discrepancy between Miller's caption and that of Conley/Campbell leads us to the Rhode Island Historical Society Library on Hope Street in Providence for a solution of the mystery.

An obvious place to begin a search for information about the departure is A Narrative of the Campaign of the First Rhode Island in the Spring and Summer of 1861, written by the regiment's chaplain, Augustus Woodbury, and published in Providence in 1862. Woodbury offers a touching description of the departure scene but makes no mention of a photograph being taken. However, pasted onto a blank page between pages 10 and 11 of the RIHS's copy of Woodbury's book is a small, two and a half inch-square paper print of an alternate view of the departure. So at least two photographs were taken on the same occasion, both of them obviously made from the same vantage point.

At least two Providence daily newspapers covered the departure of both detachments of the 1st Rhode Island and published detailed accounts. No mention is made of a photograph being taken when the first detachment left on April 20. However, the "Providence Daily Post" of Thursday morning, April 25, described the departure of the second detachment the previous day: "The last half of the First Regiment R.I. Detached Militia took its departure for New York, en route to Washington, on Wednesday afternoon...There was a dress parade on Exchange Place at nine o'clock in the forenoon, and at two o'clock in the afternoon the Battalion met at the same place to form in line and march to the steamer Empire State, which awaited them at Fox Point. The line was formed by Acting Adjutant Eddy, and reviewed by Lieut. Col. Pitman. The companies were then wheeled into platoons and remained in position a few minutes, while a daguerreotype was taken from the roof of Gorham's building, on Canal Street." "The Providence Daily Evening News" of the same date confirms the Post's account, noting that after the companies were formed in line, "A daguerreotype of the scene was then taken. The strains of Gilmore's Band, which was present as a regimental band, were very fine"—thereby identifying the band seen at the head of the column in the "En Avant" photograph (as one popular reproduction of the photo is titled).

The newspaper accounts confirm the Conley/Campbell caption is correct—the photograph (and its alternate) was taken on April 24 during the departure of the second detachment of the 1st Regiment. And if the papers' accounts are correct, we also know that the photograph was made as a daguerreotype. But while the correct date has been established—after many years of error—a number of other questions remain. Who was the photographer? At this point, unknown. Where are the original daguerreotypes? Not known to be extant. Why did Woodbury choose the alternate view to appear in his history? Good question—it isn't as evocative of the scene as "En Avant." (It's my conjecture that the Woodbury view was taken first, before the crowd built up and the troops formed in line.)

A couple of legends about the photograph have grown. When I examined several copy prints at the Rhode Island Historical Society Library, Denise Bastien, Curator of Graphics, told me that someone claims an ancestor, a certain Crocker, took the original photographs. While several Crockers are listed in the 1861 Providence city directory, none are found among the twelve individuals or firms recorded as making ambrotypes, daguerreotypes, or photographs. Ms. Bastien also noted that one of the two top-hatted figures standing next to the railing on the bridge sidewalk is believed to be Jabez Gorham. The Gorham and Company silversmiths were located at 12 Steeple Street (which fronted on Canal Street)—the building from which the photograph was taken, and which "Gorham" and his companion face in the picture, their backs to the pageant unfolding on Exchange Place.

To answer a question raises a host of other questions. Let's turn the focus to the people in the picture—sons, mothers, brothers, sisters, fathers, friends. Chaplain Woodbury remembered, "It seemed as though almost the entire population of the State of Rhode Island crowded the streets of Providence to witness the departure of this gallant band of soldiers, and to bid them God-speed upon their dangerous enterprise. The wharves, the heights upon the shores of the harbor, and the coasts of Narragansett Bay, were crowded with spectators. Cannon belched forth its thunder. Cheers of men rent the *air. The prayers and blessings of tearful women consecrated the hour. As the steamer, in which the command had embarked, left the bay, and entered upon the waters beyond, the boom of the heavy columbiads upon the parapet of Fort Adams announced to those upon the sea and those upon the land, that the shores of Rhode Island had been left, perhaps forever, by the flower of her youth and the prime of her manhood."*

Mr. Dunkelman's findings have not been questioned, and why should they, as he presents hard evidence that is difficult to repudiate. The question remains: if Dunkelman had not uncovered the misidentification of the photograph, how long would it have taken before another individual stumbled on the misidentification and had it corrected? The answer: maybe never.

What other Civil War photographs are out there filling books, magazines and albums that need further investigation—ten, twenty, a few hundred or more? Perhaps we will never know.

Part VI
TRIBUTES IN BRONZE AND STONE

MONUMENTS AND MEMORIALS ON THE BATTLEFIELDS

Rhode Islanders fought in virtually every major battle in the Civil War, including many lesser-known skirmishes. In an effort to remember their contributions during the war and pay tribute to the sacrifices of the dead and wounded, Rhode Island veterans organizations and state officials were resolute in their desire to place monuments and memorials at appropriate sites where battles were contested. Veterans groups worked diligently to raise money for the projects. However, accumulating sufficient funds from state coffers, private donations and war veterans took years, sometimes decades.

When the federal government set aside land for national cemeteries and battlefield parks, it queried the states about their interest in placing monuments at strategic locations. Most Northern states and a number of Southern states—even though the now defunct Confederacy was financially strapped—decided to take advantage of the opportunity. What evolved were three distinct types of military monuments: those that honored specific state regiments, state-supported monuments for all volunteers regardless of branch of service or unit served and monuments honoring the contributions of specific individuals, although some never served in the military (e.g., Nurse Clara Barton).

An initiative that started slowly in the mid-1870s eventually took on a life of its own. Those who have had the privilege of visiting the Gettysburg battlefield understand. Everywhere a visitor turns, a monument stands nearby. Gettysburg alone boasts 1,328 monuments, markers and memorials. To view each and read the inscriptions would be a daunting task. To a much lesser extent, the same holds true about viewing Rhode Island monuments at various battle sites. They are numerous, and there is simply not enough print space to display and explain each and every image in this book. Thus, only a sampling of battlefield monuments and memorials will be addressed here. Hopefully, the author's selection will pique the reader's interest.

New Bern, North Carolina

Still a colonel in May 1862, Ambrose E. Burnside devised a plan to invade North Carolina by reducing the forts and capturing Confederate troops on Roanoke Island. He would proceed to the city of New Bern, where the Union army planned to capture a strategic railway junction. The military operation became known as the Burnside Expedition. For Burnside and his men, the operation succeeded—one of the few times in the war when Burnside's objectives were achieved with barely a hitch. Because the colonel

and his Rhode Island boys made a vital contribution in achieving victory over the Confederates, after the war it seemed appropriate to mark the victory by placing a monument at a site near the city. That is exactly what the State of Rhode Island did.

Rhode Island's monument at the New Bern National Cemetery in New Bern, North Carolina. *Library of Congress.*

Four monuments have been erected at the New Bern National Cemetery. Two honor specific regiments: the Fifteenth Connecticut Volunteers Monument and the Ninth New Jersey Volunteers Monument. There are also two state-sponsored monuments: the Massachusetts Monument and the Rhode Island Monument. Honoring all state volunteers who died in North Carolina during the Civil War, the Rhode Island Monument was dedicated on October 6, 1909. Designed by William W. Manatt of Providence, the monument consists of a granite base topped by a bronze sculpture. Most of the graves in the cemetery are reinterments from surrounding areas such as Beaufort, Hatteras and other areas along the coast. The cemetery includes a separate section with more than one thousand unknowns.

Antietam

September 17, 1862, proved to be the bloodiest day of the entire Civil War. Both sides suffered terribly. Although General Lee's army experienced fewer casualties during the three clashes that day, the Confederate losses in the various engagements equated to a quarter of his army. The North won the battle, but barely. Rhode Islanders were well represented on the field that day. They included the Second Regiment Rhode Island Volunteer Infantry and the Fourth Regiment Rhode Island Volunteer Infantry, as well as five artillery batteries: Batteries A, B, C, D and G of the First Rhode Island Light Artillery. Batteries B and C were held in reserve, while batteries A, G and D provided artillery support and were later praised for their valor. The Second Regiment of infantry saw limited action, while the Fourth was engaged with the enemy for about ten hours under constant shelling. The Fourth lost ninety-three men killed or wounded.

Today, visitors to Sharpsburg, Maryland, cannot help but notice the monument at the center of the Antietam National Cemetery. Here stands a colossal structure measuring over forty-four feet high and weighing in at 250 tons. The base is made of twenty-seven pieces of granite, while the statue is of two large pieces of bronze joined at the waist. It is called the Private Soldier Monument but is also lovingly referred to as "Old Simon." The monument is engraved with the following words:

Not for themselves but for their country
September 17, 1862

Designed by Hartford, Connecticut architect James G. Baterson, the bronze statue was sculpted by James Pollette of Westerly, Rhode Island. The monument cost more than $32,000 to design, sculpt, stone-cut and assemble. Although the monument was erected to honor all Union soldiers who fought at the Battle of Antietam, Rhode Islanders can take pride that "Old Simon" came from the Rhode Island Granite Works.

Sculpted by James Pollette of Westerly, Rhode Island, workmen finish the Private Soldier Monument, from a period stereo view. *O. Langworthy & Company, Ashaway, Rhode Island, by C. Seaver Jr., circa 1876.*

There is also a personal monument at Antietam dedicated to Brigadier General Isaac Peace Rodman, who was mortally wounded in the engagement on September 17, 1862. His is one of six mortuary cannons mounted in stone that mark the approximate location where each Union general was killed. Each cannon has a plaque engraved with the general's name and the specifics of the incident mounted on the breach of the inverted piece.

Brigadier General Rodman lingered for several days before dying on September 30 at the age of forty. He was the highest-ranking officer from Rhode Island killed in the Civil War. His story and his final resting place are discussed in a subsequent section.

Vicksburg

During the Vicksburg Campaign, only one Rhode Island regiment was present: the Seventh Regiment Rhode Island Volunteer Infantry. And what a regiment! It fought in several clashes during the siege, all of which were marked with great gallantry. Although weakened by previous battles

The Rhode Island Monument at Vicksburg, Mississippi. *From* Report of the Rhode Island–Vicksburg Monument Commission to the General Assembly.

and illnesses, the men of the regiment managed a ferocious fight with the defenders of Vicksburg. With the help of a New Hampshire regiment, the Seventh also destroyed five hundred yards of railroad tracks and cut and burned telegraph lines near Vicksburg that were critical to the Confederacy in the West.

After receiving permission from the secretary of war for the placement of a commemorative monument, Rhode Island made its plans to place a monument at the Vicksburg Military Park in Vicksburg, Mississippi. On July 25, 1906, the Rhode Island–Vicksburg Monument Commission was created. Shortly thereafter, sculptors, artists and monument manufacturers were invited to "submit competitive designs." In November of the same year, the commission selected Frank Edwin Elwell's design. Elwell's studio was in Weehawken, New Jersey. One of the specifications was that the statue be erected on a base of granite from Westerly, Rhode Island. Elwell agreed to the stipulation and with the approval of the commission was given a contract on May 1, 1907.

When the monument was nearly complete, the following inscription was engraved on the front of the granite pedestal:

Rhode Island
7ᵗʰ Infantry
Col. Zenas R. Bliss
1ˢᵗ. Brigadier 2ⁿᵈ Div.
9ᵗʰ Corps.

Rhode Island's state seal was also affixed to the back. The negotiated price for the monument was $4,500, a figure thought to be "meager" at the time.

The bronze statue was finally completed in early March 1908 and then transported to Rhode Island to be placed on a temporary pedestal for viewing by members of the Seventh Rhode Island Veterans Association along with the general public (the permanent pedestal had previously been shipped to Vicksburg).

When the statue finally arrived in Vicksburg, it sat until cooler weather prevailed as a kind gesture to aged veterans who would take part in the official unveiling. A date was chosen, and the statue was mounted to the pedestal. The dedication of the monument took place on Wednesday, November 11, 1908. In attendance were a number of Rhode Island veterans, politicians, schoolchildren from Vicksburg and local dignitaries from the southern city. The governor of Rhode Island (the Honorable James H. Higgins) and the governor of Mississippi (the Honorable E.F. Noel) were also in attendance. After the invocation and benediction, local schoolchildren sang "America." The official unveiling, presentation and acceptance of the monument were next on the agenda. The ceremonies closed after the local schoolchildren sang "Dixie" followed by benediction by a member of the clergy.

Gettysburg

Only one Rhode Island infantry unit was engaged at Gettysburg: the Second Regiment Rhode Island Volunteer Infantry. There were also five artillery batteries from the First Rhode Island Light Artillery (A, B, C, E and G). Also contributing to the Union cause were three Rhode Islanders who served as artillery commanders for the Second, Third and Sixth Army Corps. They were Captain John G. Hazard, Captain George E. Randolph and Colonel Charles H. Tompkins. The Second Regiment saw action mostly on July 2, 1863, to help reinforce an endangered left wing.

But the real heroes from Rhode Island proved to be the men of the artillery batteries. At about 6:00 a.m. on the second, Battery A was placed along

A period engraving: Battery B Monument at Gettysburg. *From History of Battery B, First Rhode Island Light Artillery.*

Cemetery Ridge, where it saw sharp skirmishing for most of the morning and afternoon. Battery B joined the lines a bit later. At 4:30 p.m., Confederate batteries opened fire on their position before the Rebels attacked. Batteries A and B commenced firing, and eventually the enemy fire diminished before coming to a complete stop.

On the following day, July 3, Battery A played a major role in repulsing the Confederates at a thicket of trees near an open cornfield. The battle that ensued—one of the most well known of the Civil War—came to be known as Pickett's Charge. Near the wall where Battery A had been placed, Brigadier General James J. Pettigrew's North Carolina troops came within twenty yards of the battery's position but never were able to break the Union lines. Battery A fired a devastating shot that opened a wide gap in the North Carolina lines, resulting in the death of a significant number of Confederate soldiers. The battery, now running low of ammunition, had to be relieved.

At the Gettysburg Battlefield Park, there are four monuments honoring Rhode Island regiments; three are artillery and the other an infantry unit. The First Regiment Rhode Island Light Artillery honored three of its artillery batteries (A, B and E). The sole monument honoring the state's infantry unit is the Second Regiment Rhode Island Volunteer Infantry. The infantry regiment of 409 men was commanded by Colonel Horatio Rogers Jr. The regiment suffered few casualties: 1 killed and 5 wounded, with 1 reported missing. Batteries A and B did not fare as well. Battery A reported 4 men killed and 28 wounded. As for Battery B, of the 103 men present, 7 were killed and 19 wounded, with 2 reported missing. Between three batteries and an infantry unit, nearly 1,000 Rhode Island men were deployed on the battlefield. Although two other Rhode Island batteries were at Gettysburg (C and G), they were held in reserve with the Sixth Corps. No monuments were erected in their honor.

MONUMENTS AND MEMORIALS IN RHODE ISLAND

Civil War battlefields were not the only sites honored with war monuments and memorials. So, too, were towns and cities throughout the country, as well as in the state of Rhode Island. The largest monument in the state was erected across from city hall in downtown Providence only six years after the end of hostilities. The massive structure commemorates members of the First Rhode Island Regiment and the Fourteenth Rhode Island Regiment Heavy Artillery (Colored). Today, the Providence Civil War Monument is part of the Rhode Island Afro-American Heritage Trail.

Within the same park square (now called Kennedy Plaza) and not far from the Providence Civil War Monument stands a colossal statue of General Ambrose E. Burnside on horseback. It is imposing and difficult to miss.

Neither the Providence Civil War Monument nor the Burnside Monument were the first to be erected in the state. The honor goes to the citizens of Woonsocket, who commissioned their project in 1868 at a cost of $5,000. The monument was officially dedicated in 1870. What makes this monument so special? Because Woonsocket did not become an independent political

Top: Dedication of downtown Providence's Civil War Monument in 1871. *Office of the Secretary of State, A. Ralph Mollis, Rhode Island State Archives.*

Left: The Burnside Monument on Kennedy Square. *Photo by the author.*

jurisdiction until 1867, one of the first acts of the newly formed Woonsocket Town Council was to commission a Civil War monument honoring thirty-nine of their soldiers who lost their lives on various Southern battlefields and also as a tribute to Woonsocket veterans who did survive.

Other exquisitely crafted monuments were erected later in towns and cities throughout the state. Cranston, North Providence, Scituate, Warwick and Westerly commissioned and dedicated theirs. Newport and Pawtucket also paid homage to their Civil War veterans with majestic monuments placed in strategic locations in their cities. Some municipalities even erected granite and bronze testimonials in various districts. In the end, nearly every state municipality followed suit.

But in noting size, it should not be construed that smaller is any less meaningful. It took Coventry more than eighty years to erect a monument. By then, all Grand Army of the Republic veterans from the state had passed on. Erected by the McGregor Camp No. 4 Sons of Union Veterans from Rhode Island, the simple stone with plaque stands as a fitting reminder of Coventry veterans who honorably served during one of our nation's most turbulent periods.

Then there were the memorials for soldiers who died on the battlefields whose remains were brought home and laid to rest in Rhode Island cemeteries. They were joined later by their comrades in arms who were privileged to live longer and fuller lives. Both governors who served the state during the Civil War era also joined these men in eternal rest.

Flanking Riverside Cemetery on the west, Butler Hospital on the east, the Seekonk River on the north and fashionable Blackstone Boulevard on the south, a two-hundred-acre plot of land in Providence was set aside and developed for use as a private cemetery in 1846. Years after its completion, Swan Point Cemetery continues to garner praise as a work of architectural genius both for its magnificent landscaping and its period sculptures. Initially developed using a "garden" concept, the plan that was implemented accentuated the gently sloping landscape with burial plots interspersed along winding roads. Enhancing the setting are a variety of trees, numerous species of flowers and well-manicured lawns and shrubs. If you think that visiting a cemetery for sheer enjoyment and ultimate relaxation is an oxymoron, you need to see Swan Point. Not just a cemetery, it resembles a park and outdoor

Opposite, top: The Newport Civil War Monument in Newport, Rhode Island. *Photo by the author.*

Opposite, bottom: The Civil War Monument in Coventry. *Photo by the author.*

General Ambrose E. Burnside rests near his wife, Mary, at Swan Point Cemetery. *Photo by the author.*

The Sprague Mausoleum at Swan Point Cemetery. *Photo by the author.*

Above: Rhode Island governor James Y. Smith (1863–66). *From* Rhode Island's Adjutant General's Report of 1865.

Right: James Y. Smith's tomb at Swan Point Cemetery. *Photo by the author.*

Gravesite of Colonel John S. Slocum at Swan Point Cemetery. *Photo by the author.*

museum, especially in the late spring and early summer. Although solemn and serene, the cemetery is also picturesque and inviting.

Buried on the grounds are many Rhode Island Civil War notables alongside those less well known. Arguably one of the most famous grave sites is that of General Ambrose E. Burnside. Originally, Burnside was to be buried in Bristol, where he first lived as a gentleman farmer after the war, but his political aspirations and successes as governor and then as a U.S. senator brought him to Providence. Here he lived his final years, and here he was buried.

Rhode Island's first Civil War governor, William Sprague IV, whose story has been previously examined, is buried in the Sprague family mausoleum in the same cemetery. Although quite large and ornate, the top of the mausoleum is a flat-surfaced grassy area that allows visitors a place of solitude along with breathtaking views of the surrounding grounds.

Not far from Sprague's mausoleum is the burial site of Rhode Island's second and last Civil War–era governor, James Y. Smith. According to one account, Governor Smith sent his own money to regiments in the field so Rhode Island soldiers could buy provisions.

Two notable Rhode Island officers who did not survive the first engagement of the war are also buried on the grounds. Colonel John S. Slocum and Major Sullivan Ballou were both killed at the First Battle of Bull Run in Manassas, Virginia. The men's remains were brought home to be interred at Swan Point Cemetery. Members of the GAR eventually erected an elaborate crypt in Slocum's honor carved with his hat, dress coat and sword resting on top of the tombstone. The selection of the burial plot is ideal. The muffled sound of flowing water of the Seekonk River can be heard and seen in the distance. Ballou's burial plot also has views of the river. After his letter to his wife, Sarah, was read on the blockbuster Public Broadcasting Corporation (PBS) television documentary *The Civil War*, Ballou's grave site had an influx of visitors. Things have quieted down since then. For those curious, Ballou's skull is still missing long after the original battlefield grave site was desecrated.

Opposite, top left: Major Sullivan Ballou's obelisk at Swan Point Cemetery. Engraved in the monument are Major Sullivan Ballou's parting words to Sarah: "I wait for you there. Come to me and lead thither my children." *Photo by the author.*

Opposite, top right: Engraving of Elisha Hunt Rhodes. *From* Memoirs of Rhode Island Officers.

Opposite, bottom: Elisha Hunt Rhodes's austere monument at Swan Point Cemetery. *Photo by the author.*

The Ken Burns PBS documentary also featured a soldier by the name of Elisha Hunt Rhodes, a Providence, Rhode Island lad who went to war as a private and ended his military career as a colonel. After the war, Rhodes became a successful businessman. According to period accounts, he never missed a regimental reunion. Rhodes died on January 14, 1917, and is buried at Swan Point Cemetery with his wife, Caroline, and other family members. Considering his illustrious credentials, his monument is far less ornate than others in the cemetery.

On a small bluff in a remote wooded area of Peace Dale, Rhode Island, adjacent to an industrial sand and gravel pit, is the Rodman Family Cemetery. Years ago, the obelisk was visible from half a mile away, but now, with all the tree growth surrounding the cemetery, it is totally hidden from view. Finding the site is not easy, and if you are lucky enough to happen upon the entryway, it is cordoned off by cable strung across a makeshift dirt road. Venturing to the cemetery must be accomplished on foot. For years, the area around the site was neglected, having been sold and resold. Recently, as a community project, local Boy Scout Troop 1 of Kingston cleared all the unwanted trees, scrub bushes, briars, poison ivy, weeds and trash from the site. The difficult project was accomplished in a single day through the hard work of these fine young men and their leaders. But why was all the attention paid to this particular site? The cemetery happened to be the final resting place of the highest-ranking Rhode Island officer to be killed in the war: Brigadier General Isaac P. Rodman. Mortally wounded by a Minié ball in the left lung during the Battle of Antietam, he died several days later. Rodman's remains were returned to Peace Dale for burial but not before his funeral was held in the Providence Statehouse; the first time that the building was used for such an occasion.

The cemetery cleanup was successful beyond anyone's imagination. But the "law of unintended consequences" quickly took hold. On a recent visit to photograph the grave site, the author saw that vandals had toppled and broken a number of monuments and headstones. What had been hidden for years by dense vegetation now became an open target for vandals. The desecration is no different than what is happening throughout the country in far too many cemeteries that cannot afford appropriate surveillance. Sometimes there is little peace to be had, even in death.

In the tiny borough of Portsmouth Grove (now called Melville), a U.S. Army General Hospital was established in 1862 (the name was changed in

Above: The Rodman family cemetery in Peace Dale. Here lie the remains of Brigadier General Isaac Peace Rodman. His wife, Sally, who died in 1899, rests at his side. In spite of the warning sign, vandals blatantly toppled and seriously damaged a number of headstones in the family plot. *Photo by the author.*

Left: An image of Brigadier General Isaac Peace Rodman. *Library of Congress.*

Cypress Hills National Cemetery, Union Burial Ground, Section B, Brooklyn, New York. *Photo by the author.*

1863 to Lovell General Hospital to honor a former U.S. surgeon general). Although the borough was small, the hospital was not. There were twenty-eight ward buildings and nearly thirty other structures erected in support of the medical facility; 292 soldiers (both Union men and Confederate prisoners) who died there were buried on the grounds and later disinterred and reburied at Cypress Hills National Cemetery, Union Grounds, Section B, in Brooklyn, New York. One unfortunate soldier, Samuel S. Whiting, a member of the Twelfth Regiment Rhode Island Volunteer Infantry who had been wounded at the Battle of Fredericksburg, lingered for thirty-three days before dying at the hospital. His remains were claimed by his family, and he now rests in peace at First Cemetery, in East Greenwich, Rhode Island.

A nurse who worked tirelessly at the hospital, Katherine P. Wormeley, served with distinction as the first lady superintendent at the institution. Highly capable, she was greatly admired by staff and patients alike. Another Good Samaritan, Benjamin J. Tilley, though inflicted with a debilitating childhood illness, managed to visit the hospital on a daily basis, bringing books and periodicals and, when there, writing letters and providing general comfort and good cheer to the patients.

Ms. Wormeley passed away at a ripe old age. Tilley died on August 25, 1865, at the age of forty-five. Both are interred at Island Cemetery, a private burial ground in Newport.

Before the hospital closed on August 25, 1865, it had served more than 12,593 patients, with one of the lowest death rates for an institution of its kind during that period. Today, there are no markers or plaques at the former site to commemorate the hospital's existence along an eleven-acre plot near the shores of Narragansett Bay.

General Burnside's Valet

The late March day was brisk and overcast, about what you would expect for that time of year in New England. I found myself walking through a private nonprofit garden cemetery in Bristol, Rhode Island, not the first but third time I had visited since I began my research for this story. I had returned to verify some previous information and ask some questions of the affable grounds superintendent. He lives with his family on the premises in a home built entirely of granite boulders and cement; it stands adjacent to an archway held aloft by two stone pillars near the entrance to the cemetery.

Recognized in 1998 by the United States Department of the Interior, National Park Service, and listed on the National Registry of Historic Places, Juniper Hill Cemetery was constructed in 1857 on farmland purchased from Levi DeWolf, a man who made his fortune in the slave trade. The historic site consists of twenty-two acres designed in a late Gothic and mission/Spanish Revival style that is striking for its simplicity and use of terrain. The result is a cemetery whose natural grandeur provides a tranquil setting for those paying their respects to the deceased. During my previous walks along its winding roads and pathways that encompass the cemetery, I could only wonder how lovely this place must be in late spring and early summer, when tree limbs are covered with leaves, shrubbery radiates stunning hues of green and plant perennials and flowers flaunt their magnificent array of colors. Although significantly smaller than Swan Point Cemetery in Providence, the grounds are absolutely stunning. Even out of season, the backdrop I encountered made me marvel; the panoramic view of the grounds is breathtaking.

Situated on a high bluff that overlooked Providence in the distance before a dense growth of trees and a century and a half of residential development obscured the view, the cemetery is small by today's standards. Interments number fewer than nine hundred. Without a map, you would be unaware that the roads and pathways once carried biblical names, as signs have long since disappeared. Buried within are two former Rhode Island governors, three U.S. senators, a U.S. representative and a prominent politician and slave trader by the name of James DeWolf (Levi's brother). Although the Internet lists the names of the most notable burials—all politicians—this writer believes that this is not an inclusive representation. One name in particular is missing, and understandably so considering when he died; he was a black man who was nothing more than a domestic servant, a valet if you will.

The gentleman's burial site is not difficult to find. But first you need permission from the superintendent to enter the grounds. After receiving the authorization to proceed, a short drive to the easternmost section of the cemetery is in order. Fewer than twenty paces from a magnificent copper beech estimated to be between 150 and 200 years old—one of several on the grounds—are the remains of a gentleman named Robert Holloway. Near him rest several of his descendants, the most recent burial having taken place in 1992. But what makes this man's legacy so special? Robert Holloway's claim to fame is that before, during and after the Civil War, he was General Ambrose E. Burnside's personal valet. The story of his life and service to General Burnside is brief due to the paucity of information about his life, but what is known is intriguing. A single word best describes Holloway's performance of duty to his employer: loyalty.

Exactly when General Ambrose E. Burnside and Robert Holloway crossed trails for the first time remains vague. Some say it was in 1850 that Burnside, then a lieutenant in the army, met Holloway while protecting mail routes in the west. (The New Mexico Territory eventually split apart to form several states, one of which became New Mexico.) Burnside, then twenty-six years old, was Holloway's junior by nearly a decade. Unlike many of his counterparts who still languished in slavery, Holloway was a free black man from Virginia.

Robert Holloway, General
Ambrose E. Burnside's
valet. *Rhode Island Historical
Society, RHi X17 276.*

The meeting of Burnside and Holloway on the western frontier seems credible, as no current evidence contradicts it. According to Ronald S. Coddington, noted author and Civil War historian, "Burnside treated Holloway with great kindness." In return, Holloway devoted himself to the domestic needs of the future general by becoming Burnside's valet. It was during these early years together—exactly when is uncertain—that Holloway also became Burnside's bodyguard. During the ensuing years, Burnside returned to civilian life in Bristol, Rhode Island, and set up a manufacturing plant to produce a breech-loading rifle known as the Burnside carbine. Holloway continued to remain at his side.

Eleven years after their initial meeting, the Southern states rebelled. With his previous military experience and strong patriotic beliefs, Burnside became the colonel of the First Regiment Rhode Island Volunteer Infantry. Bound by duty, Holloway followed Burnside to Bull Run in Manassas, Virginia. The resultant battle proved a stunning victory for the Confederacy and a resounding defeat for the Union. Sometime during the battle and most likely during the Union's chaotic mass retreat back to Washington, Holloway became separated from Burnside and was captured by Confederate soldiers. Burnside grieved over the loss and was determined to do all possible to secure Holloway's quick release.

Holloway was taken to Richmond, where he became a cook in a Confederate prison. When word got back to Burnside as to Holloway's whereabouts in December 1861, he sent a communiqué to the Confederate government asking for Holloway's release. Previously, General George McClellan had released a number of captured Confederate servants earlier the same year. But Burnside heard nothing. Then, on February 8, 1862, with Burnside now a general and in command of an amphibious expedition on the North Carolina coast, four Confederate staff officers held as prisoners of the Union lobbied Burnside for the return of their servants separated in the same manner Burnside had lost Holloway. Burnside complied. When the jubilant officers had their servants returned, they petitioned the Confederate secretary of war, Judah P. Benjamin, for reciprocity and, specifically, the release of Holloway. This time, the Confederacy agreed to the exchange.

Robert Holloway had spent about ten months in captivity. One would surmise that after not seeing his wife, Mary, and his son and daughter back home in Bristol, he would journey to Rhode Island. But he did no such thing. Instead, he boarded a steamer destined for North Carolina to meet up with Burnside. On March 9, 1862, they were reunited on the steamship *Alice Price*.

Holloway remained with Burnside for the remainder of the general's commission in the army. After he suffered stunning defeats at Fredericksburg and Antietam, the last straw came at Petersburg in 1864 at the Battle of the Crater. What could have been Burnside's military redemption turned into a disgrace. For his performance at the Crater, Burnside's less than illustrious career as a general was finally ended when a court of inquiry censured him and four other high-ranking officers. Less than a year later, the Congressional Joint Committee on the Conduct of the War exonerated Burnside, but it was too late. The damage to Burnside's reputation was irreversible. Burnside had already returned to Bristol with Holloway at his side, knowing that his military career was over.

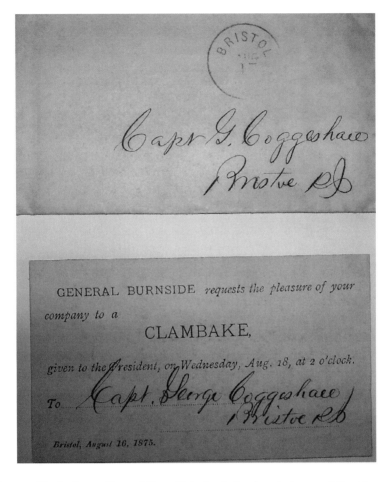

Envelope and invitation to General Burnside's clambake given in honor of President Ulysses S. Grant. *Bristol Historical and Preservation Society.*

Back in Bristol, the now retired general bought a farm, where he resumed civilian life. (The land eventually became the site of a Nike antiaircraft missile battery during the Cold War and, most recently, a university parking garage.) On his land overlooking the bay, Burnside built a two-story house, including accommodations for guests he wished to entertain.

Originally from Indiana and now a full-fledged New Englander, Burnside quickly became enamored of clambakes, including all the festivities that make such events memorable. On one occasion, he invited President Ulysses S. Grant. Grant was quick to accept the invitation. The clambake commenced at noon and lasted until midnight, and according to published reports, President Grant had a delightful time at the picnic. For several years after, Holloway took pride in showing the room where President Grant slept off the effects of libations at what must have been the mother of all clambakes.

Where Burnside failed as a commander, he succeeded as a Rhode Island politician. After the war, he was elected governor by a large majority and later became a U.S. Senator. All the while, Holloway remained at his side. But in early 1877, at the age of sixty-three, Holloway passed away. He was laid to rest in a family plot that some say was originally intended for Burnside—the general had been an active member of the Juniper Hill Cemetery Commission since its charter in 1864, but he relinquished his duties about the time he departed for Providence to serve as governor.

The retired general outlived his valet by only four years. After Holloway's passing, his son, Robert—"Robbie," as he was affectionately called—cared for the retired general, who was now dying. Burnside would be buried at a larger cemetery more befitting his stature as a retired major general and governor of Rhode Island.

Holloway's allegiance to Burnside did not go unrecognized. In 1886, on Decoration Day (now known as Memorial Day), the Bristol Chapter of the Grand Army of the Republic marched in inclement weather to the town hall, and there, the members recited the names of 125 deceased comrades who served Bristol, Rhode Island, during the war. Of course, General Burnside's name was mentioned, but in an unexpected tribute, Robert Holloway's contribution to the cause was also noted by the reading of his name. It was a fitting end to a glorious ceremony. Indeed, Robert Holloway will always be remembered as a caring soul who understood the true meaning of friendship and loyalty.

Engraved on Holloway's headstone are these words:

ROBERT HOLLOWAY,
Died Feb. 14,
1877.
Aged 63 years

For 30 years a faithful servant to
GEN. BURNSIDE,
at Home and in the Field

Grave site of Robert Holloway, Juniper Hill Cemetery, Bristol, Rhode Island. *Photo by the author.*

Robert Holloway's descendants still live in Rhode Island but carry his married daughter's surname: Strong. On occasion, family members still pay their respects at the burial site. Rest in peace, Robert Holloway. You performed your duties with the utmost courage and conviction.

Part VII

STRANGE HAPPENINGS

PECULIAR COINCIDENCES

In June 2012, the story featured below won the *Civil War Monitor* magazine's "Weirding the War" essay contest. The author attests that the actual events in the story happened and in the sequence presented. Here is the winning entry:

> *While writing about a Civil War hospital formerly situated in Rhode Island, something happened that made me realize my efforts were not in vain. It was in June 2009 when my daughter first relocated to Brooklyn, New York. Unbeknownst to her, she had moved within six miles of Cypress Hills National Cemetery where the remains of 292 soldiers that died at a Rhode Island Civil War hospital had been reinterred. She was also unaware that the present occupants of the only surviving structure* [where written provenance has survived that ties it directly to the hospital complex] *had been born in Brooklyn.*
>
> *Months later, she and I visited the cemetery. After finding the site, we parked behind a truck from Rhode Island.* Rhode Island, *I thought;* can't be. *After exchanging pleasantries with the owner of the vehicle, I learned that the gentleman actually hailed from my hometown and was visiting the cemetery to photograph headstones for a website. What are the*

odds: we came from the same town, went to the same cemetery for the first time, and arrived on the same day—both with the same purpose in mind?

There's more. After visiting the state archives to verify source data, a previously unviewed file was brought to my attention. Within it was a single letter from Albert Reeve, a steward who had served at the hospital. Here's the kicker: a few days prior, my daughter had moved to another Brooklyn apartment at Reeve Place.

Some might say, "All the coincidences relate to your daughter and only indirectly to you." They would be right had the coincidences ended there. They did not.

While finalizing my research, I learned about a collection of letters written by an invalid from the hospital. After arriving at the collector's home, I was handed a binder. Upon opening it, two words immediately grabbed my attention. No, it can't be, I thought, as shivers ran up my spine. The words were the home locale of the author of the letters: Webster, Massachusetts. What's so remarkable about that? You see, I, too, was raised in Webster and like the convalescent who wrote the letters, I also served in a war—only a century later. After reading more, I was astonished to notice several requests by the veteran to have his parents send the hometown newspaper, The Webster Times, *to him. While serving in Vietnam, my parents had done the same for me. He and I both found the newspaper a welcomed respite.*

While reflecting on these usual events, I wondered: Perhaps there's something to it; maybe I was called through some rather extraordinary means to recognize these forgotten souls.

Although the story ended there, the coincidences did not. Near completion of this manuscript, my wife and I visited a clothing store in a shopping center a few hours from home. Upon entering, my eyes caught a sign that attracted my attention: "All cloths on this rack 60% off." I walked over and pulled an army-green polo shirt off the rack. To my astonishment, the logo printed on the front breast pocket area noted, "Spring Lane Hunt Club, Tyrone, PA." I have never been to Tyrone, Pennsylvania, and could not tell anyone where it is located within the state. What I do know, however, is that I featured a photograph of a puffy-eyed Union soldier in my hospital book who had been seriously injured by a projectile. His vision was lost for life. Although the image was ghastly, I felt that showing it would make another point about the cruelty of war. And what was the coincidence? The handsome young man in the image hailed from Tyrone, Pennsylvania. Today, he lies at rest in one of Tyrone's cemeteries.

What do you think? Are the events described here simply a series of remarkable coincidences, or is something quite extraordinary happening?

CONFEDERATE PRIVATE SAMUEL POSTLETHWAITE'S FINAL RESTING PLACE

In Greenwood Cemetery, Coventry, Rhode Island, lie the remains of Confederate private Samuel Postlethwaite. During his lifetime, Postlethwaite served with Company D, Twenty-first Regiment Mississippi Infantry, with which he saw considerable action during the war. Besides his name, rank and regiment, the bronze plaque marking his grave simply notes: "Born April 6, 1833—Died August 20, 1876." In recent years, a new marker was placed there by the Department of Veterans Affairs "to recognize his service as an American soldier." But how did a Confederate veteran end up buried in a Rhode Island cemetery?

The story begins in 1990 when Les Rolston, a Rhode Island resident, went looking for a grave of a Confederate soldier. How did he know a Confederate soldier was buried in Rhode Island? He happened to read about it in an early 1960s Civil War guidebook compiled by the state. With curiosity aroused, Rolston ventured to the cemetery, but his initial search went unrewarded. In fact, it took Rolston several years before he discovered Postlethwaite's grave. He didn't find it walking through the cemetery; the information was gathered from a 1904 ledger book documenting grave sites in Rhode Island. Page 213 included a transcription for the William Rogers Greene headstone. Handwritten on the bottom of the page were the words "marble...SP." It meant that another stone of marble was nearby, and the occupant of the plot had the initials "SP." Eureka! Rolston knew that he had located the grave site because his previous research had determined that Greene was Postlethwaite's brother-in-law. Further, Rolston had already discovered that the original grave marker was simply inscribed with Postlethwaite's initials. Venturing back to the cemetery, Rolston eventually found Greene's burial site. Next to it was an open space that gave every indication of being a grave site, although the stone was missing. Over the years, the original grave marker had disappeared.

Now that Postlethwaite's resting place had been found, Rolston was determined to learn more about the Confederate. After painstaking research, numerous trips down south and lengthy phone calls, he not only solved the mystery but also was able to piece together the life of the man.

After the war, William Greene was sent down south to act as a purchasing agent for a mill his father owned in Coventry. By chance, Green happened to stay at a boardinghouse where Samuel Postlethwaite's sister, Mollie, was also a guest. Samuel was an invalid, having suffered serious wounds while fighting at the Battle of Malvern Hill during the Peninsula Campaign, and because of that, Mollie detested "Yankees."

After talking with Postlethwaite's descendants, Rolston learned that on one particular day, Mollie was eating in her room when she heard children laughing outside. Looking out the window, she spotted Greene with two children perched on each shoulder, snorting like a horse as he galloped down the dirt road. Then and there, Mollie had second thoughts about the Yankee. *Maybe he's not so bad, after all*, she reasoned. The short version of the story is: they fell in love, and before long, they became engaged.

In 1875, Greene and his wife, along with brother-in-law Samuel, returned to Rhode Island to set up residence. But Samuel was a very sick man, and because of his weakened condition, Mollie had assumed full responsibility for his care. But the end came fast. A year later, Samuel died. Not only had he suffered from war injuries, he had also contracted consumption (tuberculosis). Ironically, William also died of tuberculosis. His death came fourteen years later.

Eventually, the Greene mill was sold, and the land was later subdivided into tract housing. It wasn't long before the burial plot was forgotten. That is, until Les Rolston came along. Not only did he write a book about the Confederate soldier and the two families who make up his story—one from the North and the other from the South—but he also managed to get the Department of Veteran Affairs to furnish a marker for the site. But that was not all. On Veterans Day in 1995, Rolston organized a dedication ceremony held at the grave site that included Civil War reenactors along with descendants of both the Greene and Postlethwaite families.

According to Rolston, Postlethwaite is the only known Confederate buried in Rhode Island. No one has yet come forward to prove otherwise. Rolston's critically acclaimed work is titled *Lost Soul: The Confederate Soldier in New England*. Perhaps in a subsequent edition it should carry the title *Remembrance: Honoring a Gallant Foe*.

FEELING A COLD CHILL

Those who know him can attest to his unblemished character, fine intellect, engaging personality and straightforward common sense. Possessing traits such as these leaves little doubt why he has come to be known throughout the community as an all-around nice guy. In short, John (not his real name) is not the type of individual prone to flights of fancy, nor can he be accused of possessing an overly active imagination. That is why this story seems so out of character. Knowing John's enviable traits, after reading about what he experienced, you may feel there is some plausibility to his bizarre story.

Originally hailing from western Pennsylvania, John moved to southern Rhode Island a number of years ago and raised a family with his wife. But before John moved to Rhode Island, he attended Gettysburg College in Gettysburg, Pennsylvania. There he received a Bachelor of Arts degree in Civil War history. Later, he attended a large southern university, obtaining a Masters of Arts degree in a similar discipline. Arguably, he is well versed about America's Civil War, especially the Gettysburg Campaign and battlefield.

In early June 2005, John and his wife traveled to Pennsylvania to attend a reunion at Gettysburg College. A habitual early riser, John always enjoyed brisk walks while contemplating the natural surroundings along his path. Waking one morning at his usual time after staying in a room on campus, he had quick and easy access to the adjacent battlefield. By 6:30 a.m., John had made his way to the Eternal Light Peace Memorial, constructed on the site of the first day's battle on July 1, 1863.

As John told it, "I remember seeing only a few people in the distance near the town and an occasional automobile driving by." Near a paved road in front of the monument, John decided to sit on a cement wall and simply contemplate the sheer beauty of the countryside. He remembered thinking that the sun had just emerged over the horizon and that by all indications, it would be another beautiful day. He felt fortunate. He recalled it being "dead quiet," and for a brief instant, he gazed over the battlefield toward Oak Ridge on the flank of Seminary Ridge, near the western end of the town.

Suddenly, something caught his eye. In the distance, hanging near the ground, a hazy cloud seemed to materialize out of thin air. "I remember," he said, "feeling a cold chill…kind of a weird feeling." *It just didn't seem right*, he remembers thinking. What made the feeling even more eerie was that John remembered seeing the bright sun clearly visible above the low-lying cloud bank just before the chill settled in. By his own estimate, the cloudy mist hovered about a quarter to half a mile away from where he was sitting. Then it happened. He heard distinct sounds of galloping horses, first faint and then more and more intense and convincing. *What is that*, he thought, trying to process something that he found difficult to comprehend.

But then there was more. First, he heard the sounds of sabers and scabbards rattling against saddles and other equipment and then muffled shouts as if human voices were echoing in the air. John was uncertain about the voices—although he heard something that sounded very similar—but he was utterly convinced about the saber and scabbard rattling. According to John, the entire episode lasted over a minute and perhaps as long as a minute and a half before the noise subsided and the haze dissipated. If others had seen and heard what John experienced, the moment might have seemed brief; for others, it could have lasted an eternity.

On the way back to the college later that morning, John took the long route home using a circular path, hoping to have a similar encounter. Nothing happened, though. After arriving back on campus and a bit shaken after his eerie experience, he decided to keep what he had seen to himself, thinking that no one would believe him. Later that day, John inquired from those in the know whether any reenactors had been practicing on the battlefield that morning. There were none.

Part VIII
150ᵀᴴ ANNIVERSARY

RHODE ISLAND AND THE CIVIL WAR
SESQUICENTENNIAL

In the introduction to their immensely popular book *The Civil War*, Ken and Ric Burns wrote, "Some events so pervasively condition the life of a culture that they retain the power to fascinate permanently." But what exactly is the attraction that draws us to this epic story about war? Is it the chivalry of the Southern infantryman dressed in disheveled clothing fighting for his homeland, the tenacity of the Union artillery soldier standing steadfast in a hail of molten metal, the melancholy eyes of plantation slaves longing for freedom, the sacrifice of hundreds of thousands who died anonymously on the battlefield or is it an undefined rationale—a moment in time—that has, for whatever reason, captivated and catapulted us to a place that dwells within our hearts and minds. Whatever the reason, no other war on this continent has created such magnetism—thousands upon thousands of books have been written and will continue to be written about battlefield strategies and military and political leaders; a self-taught, gangly and homely man has been placed on the highest of pedestals; an old general with white hair and beard is admired by Southerners and Northerners alike; and men who fought and died on the field of battle, whose names are long forgotten, are still respected for their unwavering dedication and unflappable courage.

There is little doubt that America's Civil War—the momentous and deadly affair that cost thousands of lives—is one of the most defining moments in our nation's history. Whatever the appeal, this conflict will long be remembered by both serious scholars and casual observers.

About 150 years have passed since the first artillery rounds were fired at Fort Sumter in the harbor of Charleston, South Carolina, that inaugurated a brutal confrontation between the North and South lasting four agonizing years. The Civil War that ensued was so haunting, momentous and transforming that the memories of the period and a nation's healing had to be celebrated—and they were *celebrated*—first on the 50th and then the 100th anniversaries. But then something happened to dampen the enthusiasm for the latest anniversary.

After considerable lobbying by Civil War enthusiasts, a bill was introduced in Congress called the Civil War Sesquicentennial Commission Act of 2009 (S. 1838). The purpose was to establish a commission to commemorate the 150th anniversary of the war from 2011 to 2015. There was little support for the initiative, and the bill languished. It was not that politicians were uncaring; there were simply not enough funds to support the effort during a time of severe budget constraints. According to Mark Collins Jenkins in *National Geographic News*, "The necessary ammunition— money—is in short supply." For the most part, and in the end, it came down to states fending for themselves.

It appears that Virginia and Pennsylvania will manage to finance a large portion of their intended programs, while New York, a state suffering from severe budget constraints, is offering little in terms of financial support. All the states plan to do something—exhibitions, lectures, movies, music, parades, reenactments and the like—but the celebration will be a far cry from the previous two. It will be a subdued 150th anniversary.

In Rhode Island, the General Assembly passed a joint resolution that created the Rhode Island Civil War Sesquicentennial Commemoration Commission. There are twenty-seven members on the commission, along with an advisory council that will recommend and institute ways to "observe and remember" Rhode Island's contributions to the war effort. The agenda is ambitious, especially considering funding limitations. Working without pay, the group intends to accomplish the following objectives:

- support projects to restore Civil War monuments;
- rededicate the Gettysburg Gun at the Rhode Island Statehouse;
- digitize Civil War–related data that will serve as an aid to scholars;
- publish appropriate Civil War–related material about Rhode Island; and
- educate students from the state about Rhode Island's contributions to the war effort

Perhaps no other person from Rhode Island is better suited to chair the commission than Frank J. Williams. Chairman Williams, a former chief justice of the Supreme Court of Rhode Island, is a celebrated lecturer, distinguished author and renowned Civil War and Abraham Lincoln scholar. His capable staff and advisors represent an immensely diverse and highly knowledgeable group of independent scholars, college students, educators, museum curators, preservationists, reenactors, librarians, authors, civic leaders and state officials. Also playing an important role is a member of the Rhode Island Sons of Union Veterans of the Civil War and the president of the Providence Branch of the National Association for the Advancement of Colored People (NAACP).

And what will be the final outcome? As it was during the Civil War, Rhode Island will do its duty with honor and integrity. The Rhode Island Civil War Sesquicentennial Commemoration Commission will accomplish its objectives and, in the end, make its citizens proud.

Reflecting on the future, however, one wonders how the 200th anniversary of America's Civil War will be observed. Arguably, there will still be a fascination with the war, its participants and the period in general, but will the next generation's priorities and financial constraints also put a damper on the festivities? Time will tell.

RESOURCE INFORMATION AND AUTHOR NOTES

PART I. IN THE BEGINNING

Miscellany

Readers desiring more detail about Rhode Island's contributions during the Civil War are encouraged to visit two Web pages: "Rhode Island Civil War Sesquicentennial" and "Providence and Civil War." Grandchamp's book, *Rhode Island and the Civil War*, and *Rhody Redlegs*, by Grandchamp, Lancaster and Ferguson affords the reader an informative and comprehensive view about Rhode Island artillery batteries and infantry regiments during and after the Civil War.

Reverend Obadiah Homes and His Unique Gift to the War Effort

To obtain additional information about Reverend Holmes, the author recommends the following two Web pages: "Obadiah Holmes Whipped for Baptist Beliefs" and "Obadiah Holmes—Unmercifully Whipped." Randy Seaver from Southern California, along with other prominent genealogists, has proven the ancestral link between Obadiah Holmes and Abraham Lincoln.

Abraham Lincoln Visits Rhode Island

Abraham Lincoln was in Rhode Island on two more occasions than those mentioned in the initial paragraph of this section. Both times, it appears that Lincoln never disembarked from the train. The reader is encouraged to learn more about Lincoln's visit to Rhode Island by viewing Christopher Martin's transcription in *Old Stone Bank History of Rhode Island*, pages 224– 27. Additional sources include the following: "Abraham Lincoln and Rhode Island," "Abe Lincoln's Visits to New Bedford, Taunton Recalled by Deacon James N. Dunbar" and the "Rhode Island Abraham Lincoln Bicentennial Commission Final Report," by Abraham Lincoln scholar Frank J. Williams—all of which are web-based. The Honorable Frank J. Williams also provided a comprehensive account of Lincoln's visit in the November 1993 *Rhode Island History Magazine* article "Candidate Speaks in Rhode Island," arguably the finest composition regarding Lincoln's visit to Rhode Island yet written.

Rallying Cries Heard Throughout the State

There are two original copies of the Constitution of the Confederate States of America: a provisional manuscript and a permanent copy. The provisional constitution is housed at the Museum of the Confederacy in Richmond, Virginia. The permanent constitution resides in the library archives at the University of Georgia. "Old Ironsides" is still in active service. Docked in Boston Harbor, the vessel holds the distinction as the world's oldest commissioned warship still afloat.

Down South

This story was first recorded in *Personal Narratives of Events in the War of the Rebellion* by the Rhode Island Soldiers and Sailors Historical Society (Seventh Series, No. 5). William E. Meyer's narrative was titled "The Sailor on Horseback." With the war raging, Meyer left the maritime trade and mustered into Troop A of the First Regiment Rhode Island Cavalry as a private. He was taken prisoner by the Confederates and eventually exchanged before mustering out as a corporal on October 28, 1864. But salt water was in his veins, and after the war, he returned to the sea, eventually rising to the rank of captain. His senior years were spent as a citizen of St. Georges, Bermuda, where he served for many years as a German consul.

Trash Talk

If given the opportunity, the reader should peruse old Union or Confederate newspapers published during the Civil War. Most large city libraries keep these newspapers available to the general public either on microfiche or microfilm. The reader will learn quickly that there were two wars being fought: "the war on the field" and "the war of words." The amount of trash talk, propaganda, extreme bias and inaccurate reporting that was read by a gullible public during the conflict is amazing.

Practical Advice to New Recruits

Articles such as this were used as fillers and syndicated in newspapers both in the North and South. Some of the information was accurate and some was not. Most of the advice was, at the very least, entertaining.

An Inauspicious Beginning

Details for this section were extracted from the regimental account *History of Battery B, First Rhode Island Light Artillery.*

The U.S. Naval Academy during the Civil War

One of the few eyewitness accounts that survive of the Naval Academy's move from Annapolis to Newport and its short-lived existence there was written by John C. Pegram, a graduate of the academy. Pegram's account is published in the book *Personal Narratives of Events in the War of the Rebellion* (Fourth Series, No. 14). His essay is titled "Recollections of the United States Naval Academy." Much information is contained in the selection, and the author offers his regrets that space limited the telling of more details from Pegram's narrative. Fred Zillian's article in the April 13–14, 2013 edition of the *Newport Daily News*, "After War Began, Naval Academy Temporarily Moved to Newport," helped to clarify timelines about the institution's initial move to Rhode Island. Zillian's account includes several interesting anecdotes about the U.S. Naval Academy that the reader will find entertaining and enlightening. The author also used reports about the pending closure of the institution that were published in the April 6, 1865 edition of the *Newport Daily News*.

John M. Hay: The Early Years

More fascinating details about John M. Hay can be obtained by reading *Life and Letters of John Hay*, vols. I and II, by William Roscoe Thayer. Although written in the flowery literary style of the period, the volumes are still crammed with meaningful anecdotes and interesting history. The John Hay Library on the campus of Brown University contains a vast inventory of books and more than 9,100 personal papers from John Hay's original collection. With a dedicated staff of research librarians, it is well worth the visit.

PART II. THE EXCITEMENT AND THE REALITY

Did She Deserve the Title "Queen of America"?

Particulars about Julia's life can be viewed on the Internet at the following Web pages: "Julia Ward Howe Biography" and "Julia Ward Howe: Biography from Answers.com." The author also made use of Ms. Howe's autobiography, *Reminiscences: 1819–1899*. The Portsmouth Historical Society's website included a wealth of information about the Julia Ward Howe exhibit at its museum, for which the author is indebted.

The Gettysburg Gun

The entire period story can be read online by visiting the "Gettysburg Gun" Web page; the narrative is by John H. Rhodes, a sergeant from Battery

B, First Regiment Rhode Island Light Artillery. Rhodes's account of the incident was first published in *Personal Narratives of Events in the War of the Rebellion* (Fourth Series, No. 19).

Case No. 721 Turns into Case No. 428: Perez A. Hopkins

A wealth of information for this story was researched by Dr. Stephen Altic, DO. Additional detail was provided by Steve Farrington, who is the husband of Perez A. Hopkins's great-granddaughter from Perez's third marriage.

The Untimely Demise of Charles T. James

The Civil War Artillery and Cannon website is recommended for further reading, especially the page "United States Patent Office: Chs. T. James, of Providence, Rhode Island: Improvement in Projectiles."

A Chaplain's Duties

For a full accounting of Reverend Denison's work as a chaplain in the military, the reader is invited to peruse "A Chaplain's Experience in the Union Army," included in the book series *Personal Narratives of Events in the War of the Rebellion* (Seventh Series, No. 5).

Finding Comfort from a Mother's Prayers

After completing his term of service as an army chaplain and giving this account to the Christian Commission, Reverend Johnathon O. Barrows became the pastor of the Congregational Church in Northampton, New Hampshire.

Our Country Is Safe in the Hands of These Men

This story was first published in the book *Christian Memorials of the War*. The tale was titled "They Ask God's Blessing."

The Valor of George Wheaton Cole

Accounts of Cole's death were first published in two books: *Heroic Incidents and Anecdotes of the Civil War in America* and *Memoirs of Rhode Island Officers*.

Death Premonitions

Stories about the life and death of Sullivan Ballou can be found in dozens of publications. A recent book, *Civil War Love Stories* by Gill Paul, offers an interesting synopsis of the man. The account of the captain's steward, Charley Rich, was extracted from a written account by William J. Burge. The narrative was first published in 1911 by Sidney Rider in *Book Notes*. Historian Henry A.L. Brown had his annotated version published in the spring/summer 2011 edition of the Rhode Island's Civil War Round Table's newsletter, the *Monthly Return*. The article was titled, "Pawtuxet Civil War Surgeon's Story (Duty, Devotion, and the Last Kiss)."

He Died of What?

Lieutenant Smith's brief biography was published in *Memoirs of Rhode Island Officers*. Information about meningitis was obtained from two Web pages: "Meningitis: Symptoms" from the Mayo Clinic and "Meningitis Symptoms" from the Meningitis Research Foundation.

A Father's Misery: Mr. Walker's Reaction to the Loss of a Beloved Son

The story of Mr. Walker's unfortunate demise first appeared in the author's book *Rhode Island's Civil War Hospital*. The original details of the unfortunate event were first reported in the May 19, 1863 edition of the *Newport Daily News*.

PART III. THE WAR CONTINUES

In the Company of One

This account was first reported in Robert Grandchamp's book *From Providence to Fort Hell*.

The Life of the Honorable William Sprague

Rhode Island had two governors with the same name: one the subject of this story and the other an uncle who served as governor from 1838 to 1839. The mansion where both Spragues were born is now the residence of the Cranston Historical Society. For this piece, the author used material from *Memoirs of Rhode Island Officers*. Also, several Web pages are quite informative, especially "The Honorable William Sprague, the Civil War Governor." The brief article was drafted by the Cranston Historical Society.

John Gordon was the last person hanged in Rhode Island. On June 29, 2011, Governor Lincoln Chaffee pardoned Gordon after legislation by the state's General Assembly sought clemency due to the extreme bias by Justice Job Durfee, who presided over the case, and the lack of credible evidence. For those interested, a 1993 book by Charles and Tess Hoffman, *Brotherly Love*, offers a full accounting of the affair.

A Day of Reckoning with the "Confederate Air Force"

This story in its entirety can be found in the regimental account *History of Battery B, First Rhode Island Light Artillery*.

Rhode Island's Ties to the Battle of Fredericksburg

For a comprehensive discussion about Kirkland's bravery that day and why one contributor holds some reservations, the reader is directed to the website Civil War Memory and the article "Is the Richard Kirkland Story True?" For additional information about the Battle of Fredericksburg and Richard Rowland Kirkland, the reader may wish to peruse the following Web pages:

"Richard Kirkland, The Angel of Marye's Heights" and "10 Facts about Fredericksburg."

A Bawdy Letter

The soldier in the story has been purposely left unidentified. The original letter—a side of war rarely seen—is in the possession of a private collector, who graciously allowed the author to use material within its pages to write this story.

Harper's Weekly *Illustrator John Reuben Chapin*

Harper's Weekly was the first American journal to publish the Sir Arthur Conan Doyle's Sherlock Holmes mystery "The Adventure of the Cardboard Box." The author is indebted to Dr. Steven Altic, DO, for finding the Chapin story and for allowing a drawing from his private collection to be reprinted here. For a more detailed account of Mr. Chapin's life from which the author extracted material for this story, the reader is encouraged to examine the Web page "Illustrated Chapin: John Reuben Chapin," by Judy Chapin Buzby, a descendant of the highly talented illustrator. Buzby's account includes an invitation to Chapin's fiftieth wedding anniversary. Designed by the illustrator, the card includes photographs of Chapin and his wife.

Just One Apple

For a full accounting of this story the author recommends perusing *History of Battery B, First Rhode Island Light Artillery*, especially pages 115–16.

Kady Southwell Brownell

There are unsubstantiated reports that Kady's mother was a camp follower. As yet, no one has proven the allegation beyond a reasonable doubt. Therefore, the author chose facts from sources with proven documentation. A superb article published in the Rhode Island Historical Society Journal *Rhode Island History*, "Sourcing a Rhode Island Legend," by C. Morgan

Grefe, was referenced extensively for this story. To a lesser extent, the 2007 book *Women during the Civil War* by Judith E. Harper provided a first-rate synopsis of Kady's Civil War experiences.

Rhode Island–Born Confederates

To learn more intriguing details about the Civil War, the author recommends Donald Cartmell's *The Civil War Book of Lists*. Those seeking more information about the military accomplishments of Lunsford L. Lomax and Lloyd J. Beall can visit a number of websites by keying in the veterans' full names on the reader's preferred internet browser.

Murphy's Law and the Capture that Led to the Incarceration of Two Rhode Island Officers at Libby Prison

For a more thorough account of Lieutenant James M. Fales's and Captain Thomas Simpson's capture and confinement in Libby Prison, the reader is advised to peruse *Personal Narratives of Events in the War of the Rebellion*.

PART IV. WAR'S END

John Wilkes Booth and Lucy Lambert Hale

Information for this story has been extracted from various Web pages, such as "History Bytes: Newport and President Lincoln," "New Lucy Lambert Hale Pic?" and "Class and Leisure at America's First Resort." Information about Booth's rendezvous with Ms. Hale in Washington, D.C., is taken from *The Lincoln Assassination Encyclopedia* by Edward Steers Jr. The illustration of the Aquidneck House register is from the Web page "John Wilkes Booth Autograph Signature: Lot 61205."

Divergent Reactions to the Great Calamity

When first hearing the story of the young boy at a monthly gathering of the Rhode Island Civil War Round Table on the evening of February 15, 2012, this story impressed not only me but also many others in attendance that evening. Since telling the story, Frankie's grandson, historian Henry A.L. Brown, has filled in a few more details about his grandfather. "I can only remember my grandfather; the old white mustache, not a little four-and-a-half-year-old boy…but the story he shared is so vivid today and the emotion and the way he shared that moment…I, too, was transported back with him (in time)." As a teenager, Henry related that his grandfather, Frank, attended a private school in Providence where he received drill instruction in preparation for a special event from none other than Elisha Hunt Rhodes. As Henry Brown looks back, he will always remember his loving grandfather, known affectionately to him as "Popsie," and the story he felt privileged to hear and pass on to other interested listeners.

Eyewitness to a Tragic Event

Henry A.L. Brown discovered Mrs. Florence A. McQuilton's eyewitness account in an old edition of the *Providence Journal*. Mr. Brown drafted a brief article about the claim for the Rhode Island Civil War Round Table newsletter the *Monthly Return*, dated March 2012. For an entertaining read, the author recommends *We Saw Lincoln Shot*. After reading the entire volume, you may wonder if the eyewitnesses saw the same tragic event, especially those who recalled the Lincoln assassination at an advanced age.

When at First You Don't Succeed…

Although there are a number of websites that chronicle General Burnside's life, some contain misinformation; therefore, the reader is advised to use discretion. The author recommends two books: *Burnside* by William Marvel and an early period account, *The Life and Public Services of Ambrose E. Burnside, Soldier—Citizen—Statesman* by Benjamin Perley Poore. For the record, Burnside's middle name was Evert, but when he enrolled at West Point, the registrar wrote "Everett." Burnside never bothered to correct the misspelling.

Renowned Shakespearian Actor's Summer Vacation Home

An excellent article by James L. Yarnall about Edwin Booth's Boothden was published in the *Newport Historical Society Journal*. The author found the article extremely useful while writing this story. If the reader wishes to learn more about Edwin's life, two books are recommended: *Edwin Booth: Recollections by His Daughter* and *Darling of Misfortune*. For those curious, Edwin Booth's voice was recorded on a wax cylinder—a new invention of the period—that was reproduced on NAXOS Records's set *Great Historical Shakespeare Recordings and Other Miscellany*. The soundtrack also includes a compilation of other notable early twentieth-century performers. Those who listened said that because of static and the low quality of the recording, Edwin's voice is "barely audible." The stained-glass window of Mary Devlin is best viewed from the inside. Try a late Sunday morning in the spring when flowers are in bloom, and be sure to read the plaque inside the chapel. As the founder of the Player's Club in New York City, the room where Booth died has been left intact in honor of his memory, and except for an occasional dusting, it remains the same as the day he passed.

The Claims of William "Billy" H. Parker

To learn more about one of the oldest settlements in Rhode Island, now celebrating its 375th anniversary, read *Historical Tracts of the Town of Portsmouth, Rhode Island* by John T. Pierce Sr.

PART V. THE LEGACY

A Small Town's Sacrifice

Not mentioned in the story, five soldiers from Troop A, Second Regiment Rhode Island Cavalry, were listed as deserters. There is no way of knowing whether these men actually deserted or were victims of poor recordkeeping.

Memorial Day

The Web page "Memorial Day History" by the U.S. Department of Veteran Affairs, Office of Public and Intergovernmental Affairs presents an excellent synopsis of the holiday. Information relating to the observance of Memorial Day by members of the Department of Rhode Island, Grand Army of the Republic, was taken from several journals published by the organization that relate to annual encampments over a period of several years.

Rhode Island Soldiers Home

The author is indebted to the late Anthony C. Ferri, whose research and writings about the history of the veterans home in Rhode Island provided much of the source material for this story.

The Last Surviving Grand Army of the Republic Veterans from the State

Information about John H. Riley was obtained from Jack Connor, who holds a special interest in Civil War history. Information about the Grand Army of the Republic and the Department of Rhode Island Sons of Union Veterans of the Civil War was obtained from numerous websites hosted on the Internet.

Question What You See

Although all of William Frassanito's books are a worthy read, the author strongly recommends starting with *Gettysburg: A Journey in Time*. Frassanito's investigative findings of how a photographer staged a number of images using the same dead Confederate's body in the vicinity of Devil's Den is a fascinating and scholarly piece of twentieth-century photographic detective work.

PART VI. TRIBUTES IN BRONZE AND STONE

Monuments and Memorials on the Battlefields

The author highly recommends the book, *History of the Rhode Island Combat Units in the Civil War*. Information about Rhode Island monuments and memorials was found at several Web pages: "New Bern National Cemetery," "Antietam National Cemetery—Private Soldier Monument," "Six Generals Killed at Antietam," "Antietam Monuments" and "Rhode Island at the Battle of Gettysburg." For the Vicksburg portion, the author referenced a pamphlet titled *Report of the Rhode Island–Vicksburg Monument Commission to the General Assembly.*

Monuments and Memorials in Rhode Island

The author relied on several documents to prepare this story, all of which are web-based: "Woonsocket Civil War Monument—Woonsocket, Rhode Island," "Notable Persons Interred at Swan Point Cemetery," "Sesquicentennial Journey in Remembrance of Brigadier General Isaac Peace Rodman" and "Remembering (and Forgetting) General Isaac P. Rodman." The Department of Rhode Island Sons of Union Veterans has included a more comprehensive collection of Civil War monuments and memorials on its website: "Monuments and Memorial Project" and "Monuments and Memorials Postcard Collection."

General Burnside's Valet

Readers are encouraged to examine a *New York Times* article by Ron Coddington posted on July 21, 2011, to the Internet: "The Capture of Ambrose Burnside's Valet." For more detail about Burnside and his Bristol, Rhode Island estate, the author recommends two books: *Mount Hope* by George Howe and Poore's *Life and Public Services of Ambrose E. Burnside.* Information regarding Robert Holloway's descendants was obtained through informal conversations between the author and the grounds superintendent at Juniper Hill Cemetery. As for the cemetery, an excellent description of the grounds is provided in the National Register of Historic Places registration form for Jupiter Hill Cemetery, Bristol, Rhode Island.

PART VII. STRANGE HAPPENINGS

Peculiar Coincidences

For a comprehensive account about the U.S. Army General Hospital at Portsmouth Grove, Rhode Island, the author invites the reader to examine his book, *Rhode Island's Civil War Hospital.*

Confederate Private Samuel Postlethwaite's Final Resting Place

For a more detailed account of the life of this Confederate soldier, the reader is invited to read Les Rolston's enthralling book, *Lost Soul.*

Feeling a Cold Chill

For this story, the author interviewed "John" on April 16, 2013. John has been an acquaintance of the author for several years. His story is told here for the first time.

PART VIII. 150ᵀᴴ ANNIVERSARY

Rhode Island and the Civil War Sesquicentennial

More detailed information about the Rhode Island Civil War Sesquicentennial Commission can be found on the following Web page: "Rhode Island Civil War Sesquicentennial." The comprehensive site also includes educational resources about the Civil War (national and statewide) and various links to local events dealing with the Civil War.

BIBLIOGRAPHY

BOOKS

Barker, Harold R. *History of the Rhode Island Combat Units in the Civil War (1861–1865)*. USA: self-published, 1964.

Bartlett, John Russell. *Memoirs of Rhode Island Officers*. Providence, RI: Sidney S. Rider & Brother, 1867.

Brockett, Linus Pierpont. *Women at War*. Philadelphia, PA: Zeigler, McCurdy, 1867.

Cartmell, Donald. *The Civil War Book of Lists*. Franklin Lakes, NJ: New Page Books, 2001.

Chenery, William H. *The Fourteenth Regiment Rhode Island Heavy Artillery (Colored)*. Providence, RI: Snow and Farnham, 1898.

Christian Memorials of the War. Boston, MA: Gould and Lincoln, 1864.

Frassanito, William A. *Gettysburg: A Journey in Time*. New York: Charles Scribner's Sons, 1975.

Good, Timothy S. *We Saw Lincoln Shot*. Jackson: University Press of Mississippi, 1995.

Grandchamp, Robert. *From Providence to Fort Hell: Letters from Company K, Seventh Rhode Island Volunteers*. Westminster, MD: Heritage Books Inc., 2008.

———. *Rhode Island and the Civil War: Voices from the Ocean State*. Charleston, SC: The History Press, 2012.

Grandchamp, Robert, Jane Lancaster and Cynthia Ferguson. *Rhody Redlegs.* Jefferson, NC: McFarland & Company Inc., 2012.

Grossman, Edwina Booth. *Edwin Booth: Recollections by His Daughter.* New York: Century Company, 1902.

Grzyb, Frank L. *Rhode Island's Civil War Hospital.* Jefferson, NC: McFarland & Company Inc., 2012.

Guttridge, Leonard F., and Ray A. Neff. *Dark Union.* Hoboken, NJ: John Wiley & Sons Inc., 2003.

Harper, Judith E. *Women during the Civil War.* New York: Taylor & Francis Group, LLC, 2007.

Heroic Incidents and Anecdotes of the Civil War in America. New York: F. Leslie, 1862.

History of Battery B, First Rhode Island Light Artillery. Providence, RI: Snow & Farnham, 1894.

Hoffman, Charles, and Tess Hoffman. *Brotherly Love.* Amherst: University of Massachusetts Press, 1993.

Howe, George. *Mount Hope.* New York: Viking Press, 1959.

Howe, Julia Ward. *Reminiscences: 1819–1899.* New York: Houghton Mifflin, 1899.

Lockridge, Richard. *Darling of Misfortune.* New York: Century Company, 1932.

Marvel, William. *Burnside.* Chapel Hill: University of North Carolina Press, 1991.

The Old Stone Bank History of Rhode Island. Vol. III. Providence, RI: Providence Institution for Savings, 1939.

Paul, Gill. *Civil War Love Stories.* New York: Metro Books, 2013.

Personal Narratives of Events in the War of the Rebellion. Providence: Rhode Island Soldiers and Sailors Historical Society, 1892–1912.

Pierce, John T., Sr. *Historical Tracts of the Town of Portsmouth, Rhode Island.* Portsmouth, RI: Hamilton Printing, 1991.

Poore, Benjamin Perley. *The Life and Public Services of Ambrose E. Burnside, Soldier—Citizen—Statesman.* Providence, RI: J.A. & R.A. Reid, 1882.

Rolston, Les. *Lost Soul: The Confederate Soldier in New England.* Orem, UT: Ancestry, 1999.

Steers, Edward, Jr. *The Lincoln Assassination Encyclopedia.* New York: Harper Perennial, 2010.

Thayer, William Roscoe. *The Life and Letters of John Hay.* Boston, MA: Houghton Mifflin Company, 1915.

Ward, Geoffrey C. *The Civil War.* New York: Alfred A. Knopf Inc., 1990.

WEB SOURCES

Answers.com. "Julia Ward Howe: Biography from Answers.com." http://www.answers.com/topic/julia-ward-howe.

Behling, Sam. "Rev. Obadiah Homes." Obadiah Holmes, RootsWeb. http:homepages.rootsweb.ancestry.com/~sam/obadiah.html.

Blanco, Juan Ignacio. "John Gordon." Murderpedia. http://murderpedia.org/male.G/g/gordon-john.htm.

Buzby, Judy Chapin. "The Illustrated Chapin: John Reuben Chapin, (1823–1904)." Isle de Grande. www.isledegrande.com.

Civil War Artillery and Cannon Home Page. "United States Patent Office: Chs. T. James, of Providence, Rhode Island: Improvement in Projectiles." http://www.civilwarartillery.com/patents/14315.htm.

Civil War Trust. "10 Facts about Fredericksburg: December 11–15, 1862." http://www.civilwar.org/battlefields/fredericksburg/fredericksburg-history-articles/10-facts.html.

Cranston Historical Society. "The Honorable William Sprague, the Civil War Governor." http://cranstonhistoricalsociety.org/governorwilliamsprague.html.

Davis, Kay. "Class and Leisure at America's First Resort: Newport, Rhode Island, 1870–1914." American Studies, University of Virginia. http://xroads.virginia.edu/~ma01/Davis/newport/newport%20history/newport_overview.html.

Department of Rhode Island Sons of Union Veterans. "Monuments and Memorial Project" and "Monuments and Memorial Postcard Collection." http://armorydoor.tripod.com.

———. "Rhode Island Department History." http://armorydoor.tripod.com/history.html.

Dunbar, James N., Deacon. "Abe Lincoln's Visits to New Bedford, Taunton Recalled by Deacon James N. Dunbar." *The Anchor*, February 6, 2009. http://www.anchornews.org/news/february_2009/february_6_2009_4.php.

Dunkelman, Mark H. "Rhode Island Civil War Generals." Rhode Island Civil War Round Table. http://www.ricwrt.com/generals.html.

Find-a-Grave. "Rhode Island Civil War Monument." http://www.findagrave.com/cgi-bin/fg.cgi?page=gr&GRid=29278206.

Gardner, Mark. "Remembering (and Forgetting) General Isaac P. Rodman." "A History Garden" blog, August 2012. http://ahistorygarden.blogspot.com/2012/08/remembering-and-forgetting-general.html.

Gettysburg—Stone Sentinels. "Rhode Island at the Battle of Gettysburg." http://www.gettysburg.stonesentinels.com/RI.php.

Graves, Dan, MSL. "Obadiah Homes Whipped for Baptist Beliefs." Christianity.com. http://www.christianity.com/church/church-history/timeline/1601-1700/obadiah-holmes-whipped-for-baptist-beliefs-11630124.html.

Haley, John Williams. "Abraham Lincoln in Providence." Quahog.org. http://www.quahog.org/factsfolklore/index.php?id=189.

Higgins, Henry. "General Charles Tillinghast James, 1805–1862." Civil War Artillery and Cannon Home Page. http://www.civilwarartillery.com/inventors/james.htm.

Jenkins, Mark Collins. "Civil Wear at 150: Expect Subdued Salutes, Rising Voices." *National Geographic Daily News*, April 7, 2011. http://news.nationalgeographic.com/news/2011/04/110407-civil-war-150th-anniversary-fort-sumter-battle.

Julia Ward Howe. "Julia Ward Howe Biography." http://www.juliawardhowe.org/bio.htm.

Lackey, Katharine. "Civil War Events Proceed Despite Lack of Funds." *USA Today*, April 4, 2011. http://usatoday30.usatoday.com/news/nation/2011-04-11-civil-war-commemoration-plans_N.htm.

Levin, Kevin. "Is the Richard Kirkland Story True?" Civil War Memory. http://cwmemory.com/2009/12/22/is-the-richard-kirkland-story-true.

Lincoln Discussion Symposium. "New Lucy Lambert Hale Pic?" http://rogerjnorton.com/LincolnDiscussionSymposium/archive/index.php?thread-357-2.html.

Lincoln Institute Presents Abraham Lincoln's Classroom. "Abraham Lincoln and Rhode Island." http://www.abrahamlincolnsclassroom.org/Library/newsletter.asp?ID=40&CRLI=120.

Live Auctioneers (Heritage/Heritage.com). "John Wilkes Booth Autograph Signature: Lot 61205." http://www.liveauctioneers.com/item/5898483.

Marvel, W. "Ambrose E. Burnside (1824–1881)." *Encyclopedia Virginia*, May 3, 2011. http://www.encyclopediavirginia.org/Burnside_Ambrose_E_1824-1881.

Mayo Clinic. "Meningitis: Symptoms." http://www.mayoclinic.com/health/meningitis/DS00118/DSECTION=symptoms.

Melton, Jack W., Jr. "Civil War Artillery Projectiles." Civil War Artillery and Cannon Home Page. http://www.civilwarartillery.com.

Meningitis Research Foundation. "Meningitis Symptoms." http://www.meningitis.org/symptoms.

Merchant, David. "Memorial Day History." U.S. Memorial Day History. http://www.usmemorialday.org/backgrnd.html.

Merka, G.A. "Ambrose Everett (Everts) Burnside Commander-in-Chief 1871/1872 and 1872/1873." Sons of Union Veterans of the Civil War National Headquarters. http://suvcw.org/garcinc/aeburnside.htm.

National Cemetery Administration, U.S. Department of Veterans Affairs. "New Bern National Cemetery." http://www.cem.va.gov/cems/nchp/newbern.asp.

National Park Service, U.S. Department of the Interior. "Antietam Monuments." http://www.nps.gov/anti/historyculture/monuments.htm.

———. "Antietam National Cemetery—Private Soldier Monument." http://www.nps.gov/resources/place.htm?id=60.

———. "Private Soldier Monument." http://www.nps.gov/anti/historyculture/mnt-pvt-soldier.htm.

———. "Six Generals Killed at Antietam." http://www.nps.gov/anti/historyculture/6generals.htm.

Newport Historical Society. "History Bytes: Newport and President Lincoln." http://newporthistorical.org/index.php/history-bytes-newport-and-president-lincoln.

Office of Public and Intergovernmental Affairs, U.S. Department of Veterans Affairs. "Memorial Day History." http://www.va.gov/opa/speceven/memday/history.asp.

Office of the Secretary of State, A. Ralph Mollis. "Civil War Monument Dedication, 1871." http://sos.ri.gov/virtualarchives/items/show/400.

Portsmouth Historical Society. "Buildings and Exhibits." http://portsmouthhistorical.com/buildings-and-exhibits.

———. "Julia Ward Howe Room." http://portsmouthhistorical.com/buildings-and-exhibits.

Rhodes, John H. "The Gettysburg Gun." Gettysburg Discussion Group. http://www.gdg.org/Research/MOLLUS/mollus14.html.

Seaver, Randy. "Happy 200th Birthday, Cousin Abraham Lincoln." Genea-Musings. http://www.geneamusings.com/2009/02/happy-200th-birthday-cousin-abraham.html.

Sons of Union Veterans of the Civil War National Headquarters. http://www.suvcw.org.

Swan Point Cemetery. "Notable Persons Interred at Swan Point Cemetery." http://swanpointcemetery.com/notable-people.php.

Szekely, Mike, Pastor. "Obadiah Homes—Unmercifully Whipped." "The Pastor's Pen" blog. http://lbcpastor.wordpress.com/2008/05/14/obadiah-holmes-unmercifully-whipped.

Urso, Lori. "Sesquicentennial Journey in Remembrance of Brigadier General Isaac Peace Rodman." Pettaquamscutt Historical Society. http://www.pettaquamscutt.org/rememberinggeneralrodman.htm.

U.S. Naval Academy. "A Brief History of USNA." http://www.usna.edu/USNAHistory.

Waymarking. "Woonsocket Civil War Monument—Woonsocket, Rhode Island." American Civil War Monuments and Memorials. http://www.waymarking.com/waymarks/WM4ZXM_Woonsocket_Civil_War_Monument_Woonsocket_Rhode_Island.

Wikipedia. "Lloyd J. Beal." http://en.wilkipedia.org/wiki/Lloyd_J._Beal.

———. "Lunsford L. Lomax." http://en.wikipedia.org/wiki/Lunsford_L._Lomax.

Williams, Frank J. "Providence and Civil War" City of Providence. https://www.providenceri.com/archives/375th-essays-providence-and-civil-war.

———. "The Rhode Island Abraham Lincoln Bicentennial Commission Final Report, June 30, 2010." http://sos.ri.gov/documents/library/RIALBC-final-report.pdf.

———. Rhode Island Civil War Sesquicentennial. http:/www.rhodeislandcivilwar150.org.

Wyckoff, Mac. "Richard Kirkland, The Angel of Marye's Heights." Fredericksburg.com. http://fredericksburg.com/CivilWar/Battle/kirkland.htm.

BULLETINS, NEWSLETTERS, PAMPHLETS, ARTICLES AND REPORTS

Achorn, Edward. "Nov. 6, 1860: The Finest Hour of Illinois's 'Little Giant.'" *Providence Journal*, November 6, 2012.

Brown, Henry A.L. "Pawtuxet Civil War Surgeon's Story: Duty, Devotion, and the Last Kiss." *Monthly Return* (Spring/Summer 2011). Rhode Island Civil War Round Table. This story first appeared in Sidney S. Rider's publication *Book Notes* 28, no. 1 (January 24, 1911).

Coddington, Ronald S. "The Capture of Ambrose Burnside's Valet." *New York Times*, July 21, 2011.

Ferri, Anthony C. "Rhode Island Soldiers Home." *Bristol Phenix*. Centennial Edition. Bristol, Rhode Island, n.d.

Grand Army of the Republic. Journals of the Forty-first, Forty-second and Forty-fifth, Annual Encampment of the Department of Rhode Island GAR, Providence, Rhode Island, 1908, 1909 and 1912.

Grefe, C. Morgan. "Sourcing a Rhode Island Legend." *Rhode Island History Journal* 70, no. 1 (Winter/Spring 2013).

Grzyb, Frank L. "The Black Soldiers of the 14th Rhode Island Heavy Artillery Toiled for the Cause of Freedom." *America's Civil War Magazine* (March 2001).

Jones, Evan C. "Sullivan Ballou: The Macabre Fate of a American Civil War Major." *America's Civil War* (November 2004).

Monthly Return 20, no. 7. "Providence Woman Saw Lincoln Shot" (March 2012). Rhode Island Civil War Round Table.

Notes for Bibliophiles. "Rhode Island Civil War Relic Discovered." Providence Public Library Special Collections. http://pplspcoll. wordpress.com/2009/02/05/rhode-island-civil-war-relic-discovered.

Rhode Island General Assembly. *The Rhode Island Statehouse: A Self-Guided Tour.* Providence, RI: self-published, 2004.

Rhode Island–Vicksburg Monument Commission. *Report of the Rhode Island–Vicksburg Monument Commission to the General Assembly.* Providence, RI: Providence Press, 1909.

Troy, George F., Jr. "Rhode Island's Boys in Blue." Series in the *Providence Journal,* May 1937.

U.S. Department of the Interior, National Park Service. National Register of Historic Places registration form, Jupiter Hill Cemetery, Bristol, Rhode Island.

Williams, Frank J. "A Candidate Speaks in Rhode Island: Abraham Lincoln Visits Providence and Woonsocket, 1860." *Rhode Island History Magazine* 51, no. 4 (November 1993).

Yarnall, James L. "Boothden (Part III)." *Newport Historical Society Journal* 68, no. 236 (November 1997).

Zbailey, Michael S. "Sarah, Never Forget How Much I Love You." *Providence Journal,* July 10, 2011.

Zillian, Fred. "After War Began, Naval Academy Temporarily Moved to Newport." *Newport Daily News,* April 13–14, 2013.

NEWSPAPER AND PERIODICALS

America's Civil War.
Bristol Phenix.
Harper's Weekly.
Newport Daily News.
Providence Journal.

INDEX

ABOUT THE AUTHOR

Frank L. Grzyb, a decorated combat veteran, is the author of three previous books: *Touched by the Dragon* (reissued in trade paperback as *A Story for All Americans*), *Ain't Much of War* and *Rhode Island's Civil War Hospital*. His work has been featured in such magazines as *America's Civil War*, *Civil War Monitor* and the *Civil War Times*. When not enjoying his family, especially his grandchildren, Frank serves as a guest lecturer at high schools, universities and military, civic and religious organizations. To further enhance his knowledge about America's Civil War, Frank is a member of the Rhode Island Civil War Round Table. Retired from government service, he and his wife reside in Rhode Island.